"From its radical beginnings in the English Civil War to its diverse, multi-ethnic global presence, this concise introduction may be the single best panorama of the Quaker world yet written. It's destined to be a standard source in the field for both scholar and general reader."
     —**Carole Dale Spencer**, *Portland Seminary of George Fox University, USA. Author of* Holiness: The Soul of Quakerism

"*Quakerism: The Basics* is an important work for anyone wanting to understand the essentials of Quakerism. In clear accessible prose, the Abbotts guide readers through Quakerism's past and present revealing the incredible diversity within the Religious Society of Friends. Strongly foregrounding voices from the Global South, this volume clearly introduces an often misunderstood religious group."
     —**Robynne Rogers Healey**, *Trinity Western University, Canada*

"In this new book covering the basics of Quakerism, Marge and Carl Abbott offer a refreshing combination of Quaker history, relevant aspects of faith and practice, and a helpful representation of the diversity of the worldwide family of Friends. Especially welcome is the featuring of emerging Quaker expressions in developing nations, illuminating how historic movements of the Spirit continue to touch the world in renewing and redemptive ways after the manner of Friends."
     —**Paul N. Anderson**, *George Fox University, USA*

QUAKERISM

THE BASICS

Quakerism: The Basics is an accessible and engaging introduction to the history and diverse approaches and ideas associated with the Religious Society of Friends. This small religion incorporates a wide geographic spread and varied beliefs that range from evangelical Christians to non-theists. Topics covered include:

- Quaker values in action
- The first generations of Quakerism
- Quakerism in the eighteenth and nineteenth centuries
- Belief and activism
- Worship and practice
- Quakerism around the world
- The future of Quakerism.

With helpful features including suggested readings, timelines, a glossary, and a guide to Quakers in fiction, this book is an ideal starting point for students and scholars approaching Quakerism for the first time as well as those interested in deepening their understanding.

Margery Post Abbott is a member of the Multnomah Meeting in Portland, Oregon and an independent scholar who has published widely on Quaker belief and practice.

Carl Abbott is a member of the Multnomah Meeting and Professor Emeritus of Urban Studies and Planning at Portland State University, USA.

The Basics

For more information about this series, please visit: https://www.routledge.com/The-Basics/book-series/B

QUAKERISM

THE BASICS

Margery Post Abbott and Carl Abbott

LONDON AND NEW YORK

First published 2021
by Routledge
2 Park Square, Milton Park, Abingdon, Oxon OX14 4RN

and by Routledge
52 Vanderbilt Avenue, New York, NY 10017

Routledge is an imprint of the Taylor & Francis Group, an informa business

British Library Cataloguing in Publication Data
A catalogue record for this book is available from the British Library

Library of Congress Cataloging-in-Publication Data
Names: Abbott, Margery Post, author. | Abbott, Carl, 1944- author.
Title: Quakerism : the basics / Margery Post Abbott, Carl Abbott.
Description: Abingdon, Oxon ; New York : Routledge, 2021. |
Series: The basics | Includes bibliographical references and index.
Identifiers: LCCN 2020029026 | ISBN 9780367191610 (hardback) |
ISBN 9780367191627 (paperback) | ISBN 9780429200816 (ebook)
Subjects: LCSH: Society of Friends.
Classification: LCC BX7731.3 .A23 2021 | DDC 289.6–dc23
LC record available at https://lccn.loc.gov/2020029026

ISBN: 978-0-367-19161-0 (hbk)
ISBN: 978-0-367-19162-7 (pbk)
ISBN: 978-0-429-20081-6 (ebk)

Typeset in Bembo
by Taylor & Francis Books

Printed and bound by CPI Group (UK) Ltd, Croydon, CR0 4YY

CONTENTS

ILLUSTRATIONS

FIGURES

TABLES

BOXES

ACKNOWLEDGMENTS

We are grateful to the members of Multnomah Monthly Meeting, Bridge City Friends Meeting, and West Hills Friends Church who met with us to discuss and critique draft chapters. Their comments kept our focus on the forest rather than the trees. Thomas Hamm, Jessica Starling, Rick Seifert, Robin Mohr, and Peter Eccles read the manuscript and saved us from more than one mistake and infelicitous expression. Esther Mombo, Eden Grace, Ronis Chapman, Nancy Thomas, Nancy Irving, Julie Peyton, and Margaret Fraser clarified points about Friends around the world. We appreciate the confidence of Quaker scholars Pink Dandelion and Steve Angell, who suggested that we consider this project, and of course the valuable comments of the anonymous reviewers.

ABBREVIATIONS

AFSC	American Friends Service Committee
EFCI	Evangelical Friends Church International
FCK	Friends Church in Kenya
FCNL	Friends Committee on National Legislation
FGC	Friends General Conference
FUM	Friends United Meeting
FWCC	Friends World Committee for Consultation
INELA	Iglesia Nacional Evangelica "Los Amigos" Boliviana
QUNO	Quaker United Nations Office
USFWK	United Society of Friends Women Kenya

INTRODUCTION

Quakers are both admired and poorly understood. Even the name can be confusing. Their formal name is either the Religious Society of Friends or Friends Church, depending on where you are in the world. So Quakers call themselves Friends with a capital F. The name "Quaker" originally began as a term of ridicule that early Friends chose to embrace and give their own meaning.

Contemporary Quakers often have to explain that no, the denomination has not died out, and no, they don't depend on horse and buggy like the Amish, despite common Pennsylvania connections. At the same time, examples of their progressive activism are cited with almost mythological reverence. These include Quaker work against human slavery, their early recognition of the spiritual equality of women, and their testimony against engaging in war. These are vivid examples of the seriousness with which many Quakers have taken Sermon on the Mount.

Quakers are distributed widely around the globe, and they experience many of the tensions of the broader church. Their numbers are small, with fewer than a half a million Friends in total. Kenya has the most, followed by the United States, Burundi, Bolivia, and then the Quaker mothership of Great Britain. The large majority consider themselves unquestionably Christian, especially in Africa and Latin America where missionaries from North America and Britain spread Quakerism beyond its European roots. In contrast, most Friends meetings in Europe and some in North America do without paid pastors, formal church services, and explicit statements of faith. This opens the way for participants whose beliefs range from Christian to non-theist or who may see themselves as Buddhist/Quaker or Jewish/Quaker.

Quakerism has changed as it has spread around the world. North American Quaker practice in the 1800s differed from the original English forms of the 1600s. Forms of worship in the United States evolved as they spread westward, creating substantial differences among Friends in centers like Pennsylvania, Iowa, and Oregon. To nobody's surprise, Latin American and African Friends have built their own traditions and practices distinct from those of the historic Quaker core in the Atlantic world.

The Society of Friends has also been marked by increasing theological variety. Early Quakers saw themselves as returning to the roots of Christianity as it may have been before the development of church institutions. Over the centuries, many Quakers have retained and reemphasized a Christian center, while others have welcomed increasing spiritual variety. At the same time, Quakerism has a durable theological core—the direct accessibility of the divine to everyone, at least potentially. Early Friends called this the Inward Light or Light of Christ. Many modern Friends speak about "that of God in everyone." The understanding of what the Inward Light calls Friends to do has changed with the character of surrounding society—challenging aristocratic pretension in 1600s, challenging slavery in the eighteenth and nineteenth centuries, making fumbling steps toward genuine racial equality in the twentieth and twenty-first centuries

This same theology means that Quaker practice has often involved women more fully in preaching and decision making than the social standards of the time might accept. This attention to women, initially as spiritual and then as practical leaders, began with the first generation and has broadened to the present. Quaker women have been a powerful force in British and American reform efforts for two centuries, and the Society of Friends remain an empowering force influencing women in Africa, Latin America, and Asia.

Members of the Religious Society of Friends have often been stereotyped by certain distinctive behaviors and customs, such as the historic use of "thee" and "thou" in speech or preference for very plain clothing. As these "distinctives" have lost their relevance and dropped away, what has remained for over 370 years is the importance of listening for guidance from the voice of the Holy Spirit within while also testing that guidance with the wisdom of the larger community. Quakerism is thus a highly individualistic and strongly community-centered religion at the same time.

Our first chapter introduces Quakerism with a series of short examples of Quaker work in the world outside the confines of their meetings (the traditional term for Quaker congregations) and churches (the common term in Africa and South America and used as well in parts of the United States). Readers will meet contemporary American, British, and African Quakers living out their beliefs and working for positive change.

Chapter 2 steps back in history to explore the first 50 years of Quaker faith and practice in England and its spread to English colonies in the New World. Quakers were among many dissenting groups and sects that formed around the time of the English Civil War (1642–8). Like other dissenters, they thought that a state church supported by government-collected taxes distorted true Christianity. They sometimes called themselves Children of the Light referring to the Gospel of John 12:36. They also called themselves Friends of Truth, referring to John 15:14: "You are my friends if you do what I command you. I do not call you servants any longer, because the servant does not know what the master is doing; but I have called you friends, because I have made known to you everything I have heard from my Father." Their adherence to the authority of the Christ as found in their own hearts and as they understood the clear teachings of Scripture, combined with their refusal to obey civil law when they perceived it to be contrary to the law of God, made them a dangerous group in the eyes of Parliament and the Church of England. By the end of the 1600s, however, Quakerism seemed on a politically safe foundation, with formal toleration in England and in Quaker-led colonies in Pennsylvania and New Jersey.

Chapter 3 follows this tumultuous beginning by detailing Quaker contradictions and contrasts in the following centuries. Many Quakers turned away from public affairs in what is sometimes called the "quietist" era of the eighteenth century. But the Society of Friends also expanded vigorously with the movement of English-speaking settlers across North America. Peculiar customs set them apart from mainstream social values, but they simultaneously played important roles in the development of industry and science. They were increasingly seen as fusty and conservative.

However, nineteenth-century Quaker women would step forth as leaders in the movements for women's rights, just as many Quakers worked for the abolition of slavery, universal suffrage, temperance, Native American treaty rights, and full rights for African Americans.

Chapter 4 traces the spread of the Society of Friends through the influence of Quaker writings, evangelism, and missionary work in Africa and South America since the early twentieth century. It addresses the differences that arise from its interaction with social and cultural environments as different as rural communities in Bolivia and university towns in the United States, and the commonalities that remain.

Variety is also the theme of Chapter 5, which describes styles of worship and practice. Members of the Society of Friends in the twenty-first century worship in multiple ways. Evangelical Quaker churches in the United States, Africa, and Latin America often employ paid pastors, and conduct worship services similar to those in a Methodist or Nazarene church. Other meetings in the British Isles, Europe, Australasia, and the United States maintain the tradition of worship out of silent waiting with every participant a potential minister. Quakers conduct the business of their church or meeting with what looks to observers as a consensus process but that is ideally a much deeper effort to come to unity as led by divine spirit.

A chapter on "faith and action" returns to the topics introduced at the start of the book, placing them in theological as well as political context. Quaker social action grew out of their reading of the Bible and interpretation of the Christian message. These roots remain vital for most Friends today, although some find their inspiration for action in other spiritual practices and approaches, particularly those that emphasize simplicity and non-violence and those that draw on reverence and protection for the natural world.

Like many religious movements, Quakers have disagreed about specifics of theology and practice. The resulting divisions now span the same spectrum of theology and values running from progressive to traditional/orthodox approaches that we find in many religious groups. Our final chapter examines the tensions that continue to divide Quakers. Many of these are modern versions of the conflict between individual leadings and the authority of the larger group that bedeviled the first Quakers. At the same time, the small numbers of Friends have motivated many to develop relationships across geographic and theological distances. This gives them the opportunity to engage one-on-one around questions that have separated not only Friends, but almost every Christian denomination.

It is useful to explain some common terms that Quakers use in ways that are sometimes obscure to non-Quakers:

- *Programmed* and *unprogrammed* refer to the style of worship. Programmed worship resembles a Protestant service with a combination of hymns, sermons, and readings from Scripture. In unprogrammed worship, Quakers gather in expectant silence out of which individuals may share thoughts and messages. Some services may be semi-programmed with substantial periods of silent worship along with planned messages and song.

- It is not easy to divide Quakers with the terms *conservative* and *liberal*, which are best used as adjectives, as with "theologically liberal" or "socially conservative." When capitalized, Conservative Friends are a small but distinct group among American Quakers. Many Quakers see themselves as *evangelical*, meaning strongly Christian in belief and committed to outreach.

- Quaker congregations may call themselves a *meeting* or a *church*. The majority of meetings use unprogrammed worship and the majority of churches use programmed worship, but there is not a one-to-one match.

We close this introduction with a word about ourselves. We both are active Friends in the tradition that is most liberal theologically and politically, but we are familiar and comfortable with the biblical references and language that were essential to early Quakers and remain central for evangelical Quakers. We have worshipped among Friends of many persuasions in nine countries on three continents. Marge is active as a teacher and workshop leader for Quakers throughout the English-speaking world, and has published or edited several books about Quaker history and belief, often including Friends worldwide. She has worked to build bridges among evangelical and liberal Quakers in the Pacific

Northwest of the United States and participated in world conferences of Friends in Kenya in 1991 and 2012. Carl has a long career as a teacher and scholar of American history and has held many roles with local and regional Quaker organizations.

In 1656, founder George Fox urged the first generation of Quakers to "be patterns, be examples in all countries, places, islands, nations wherever you come; that your carriage and life may preach among all sorts of people, and to them; then you will come to walk cheerfully over the world, answering that of God in everyone; whereby in them you may be a blessing, and make the witness of God in them to bless you." We believe that the Society of Friends, with its distinctive understanding of Christianity, has much to offer individuals as they seek God, It also has much to offer the world. These contributions can be most useful when we appreciate the evolution of Quakerism over the centuries, its diversity, its flaws, its failures, and its successes.

LIVES LED BY THE SPIRIT
ACTION GROUNDED IN FAITH

The Religious Society of Friends values both inward spiritual life and its outward expression in the world. In the ideal, Quakers do not wait for charismatic leadership but instead approach the world as everyday prophets who follow personal and communal leadings to promote social justice in the communities where they live. They seek to listen for the inward guidance of the Light of Christ not only in worship, but also in their day-to-day lives. This spiritual guidance offers a counter-balance to broader cultural pressures to amass individual wealth and power.

In 1985, young adult Quakers from around the world came together for the World Gathering of Young Friends, an intense week of sharing and worship on the campus of Guilford College in Greensboro, North Carolina. Some came from "meetings" where there is no formal worship service and no explicit statement of faith. Others came from "churches" that have much in common with the less formal Protestant denominations. Their epistle or closing statement noted their diversity: "We have come together from every continent, separated by language, race, culture, ways we worship God, and beliefs about Christ and God … We have been challenged, shaken up, at times even enraged, intimidated, and offended by these differences in each other. We have grown from this struggle and have felt the Holy Spirit in programmed worship, singing, Bible study, open times of worship and sharing, and silent waiting upon God." The experience transformed many participants and sparked a new generation of leadership in the Religious Society of Friends. These young Quakers were often transformed by the passionate differences they encountered.

They were also impatient with their elders and found an underlying unity despite differences of both belief and practice.

> We have often wondered whether there is anything Quakers today can say as one. After much struggle we have discovered that we can proclaim this: there is a living God at the centre of all, who is available to each of us as a Present Teacher at the very heart of our lives. We seek as people of God to be worthy vessels to deliver the Lord's transforming word, to be prophets of joy who know from experience and can testify to the world, as George Fox did, that the Lord God is at work in this thick night! ... It is our desire to work co-operatively on unifying these points. The challenges of this time are almost too great to be faced, but we must let our lives mirror what is written on our hearts—to be so full of God's love that we can do no other than live out our corporate testimonies to the world of honesty, simplicity, equality and peace, whatever the consequences.

Attention to the divine spark as a guide for the tasks of daily life forms the foundation for Friends' witness in the world. They believe strongly that the result of this attention should be visible in their words and deeds. Some may describe it as striving to build communities governed by nonviolence and equality. Others may understand it through the message of Matthew 25 that to care for the poor and the hungry is to care for Christ. Such inward guidance can bring Quakers into sharp conflict with cultural values of accumulation of wealth, desire for fame, and taste for aggression. Quaker witness to the love of God takes many forms. The willingness to wait for guidance from the Inward Light can give courage and strength and open hearts to creativity.

THE ROOTS OF QUAKER SOCIAL WITNESS

> And when all my hopes in them [priests] and all men were gone, so that I had nothing outwardly to help me, nor could tell what to do, then, Oh then, I heard a voice which said, "There is one, even Christ Jesus, that can speak to thy condition" and when I heard it my heart did leap for joy ... My desires after the Lord grew stronger, and zeal in the pure knowledge of God and of Christ alone, without the help of any man, book or writing.

(Fox 1952, p. 11)

This short passage by George Fox is the formative statement for the Society of Friends. Fox was a young Englishman who wandered the countryside "as a stranger on the earth" seeking for a faith more powerful than what he found in the existing churches. In 1647, at age 23, he had the deep religious experience that he articulated in the words quoted above. Following this new sense of divine leading during a time of civil upheaval in England, Fox encountered many other seekers hoping for renewal of the church. In 1652, considered the founding date of Quakerism, Fox was traveling in the rugged northwest corner of England. Climbing more than a thousand feet to the top of Pendle Hill, he had a vision of "a great people to be gathered" who saw Christ as their one teacher. They were to be great in numbers, great in passion for God, and great in their willingness to live Christ-guided lives. Weeks later, he preached to a thousand seekers on Firbank Fell near the town of Kendal, inspiring and launching Quakers as a religious movement.

Quakers worked to influence government from their start. Church and state were intertwined in mid-seventeenth-century England. The state enforced the collection of tithes to support the clergy and often elaborate houses of worship, and it required everyone to attend the state church. In their witness that Christ had come to teach his people himself, Quakers believed that neither priests nor Scriptures were needed to mediate between God and humanity. Their non-payment of forced tithes was at once a protest against a corrupt system and an assertion that tithing to the church was to be freely given.

The first years of Quakerism were a time of turmoil punctuated by civil war, the beheading of Charles I, the establishment of the Protectorate under Oliver Cromwell, and then the restoration of the monarchy with Charles II in 1660. Plague took a massive death toll in 1665. A fire nearly destroyed London in 1666. Quakers were one of many dissenting groups that sought to establish the right to worship according to their own consciences and that advocated for economic and social justice. They hoped to see the kingdom of God established in England in their lifetimes. Many of these dissenters had fought against the king under Oliver Cromwell but were sorely disillusioned once Cromwell was in power, losing hope that arms would bring about God's kingdom.

The Quaker response was unusual. Friends in England and later in the American colonies advocated nonviolent change, believing that "dissent thus should be a process of persuasion and convincement, not coercion" (Calvert 2006, pp. 66–7). Margaret Fell, a co-founder of Friends and active lobbyist on their behalf, asserted that love was at the heart their actions. Quakers stated their loyalty to the government even as they asserted the limits to that loyalty when the laws violated the clear leadings of Christ.

In 1660 Fell sent the king and Parliament a key defense of the Quaker position: "A Declaration and an Information from Us, the People of God Called Quakers." George Fox and a dozen other prominent Quakers endorsed the statement. It directly linked the refusal of Friends to swear oaths, to worship in the Church of England, and other radical actions to the teachings of Jesus. She argued that the many who were in prison were not a threat to the kingdom. Their protest was against unjust laws, particularly the law mandating a state religion. In their own defense Friends looked to Acts 16 and the example of Paul, who was beaten and imprisoned but accepted the punishment, even refusing to walk away when an earthquake broke open the prison walls. Fell stated that Friends' imprisonment was not a result of any evil-doing or wish to harm others, "but for con-science's sake towards God." She continued "we are a people that follow after those things that make for peace, love and unity. It is our desire that other's feet may walk in the same. For no other cause but love to the souls of all people have our sufferings been" (Wallace 1984, p. 54).

A clear theme of Fell's "Declaration" was the understanding that obedience to the state was secondary to obedience to God. This stance that government was not to hinder worship or dictate its form became fundamental to the laws of Pennsylvania as established by William Penn, one of the most important of the second generation of Quakers.

The focus of early Friends on God's love becoming visible in human acts of compassion and justice continues to lead individual Quakers and Quaker organizations. Their actions have sometimes set them apart *and* expanded their influence beyond their numbers. Quakers call the public expressions of their beliefs and behaviors "testimonies" because they testify to the experienced leadings of God. The people we highlight in this chapter show the continued vitality of the approach to public service and political action that Margaret Fell articulated. The examples do not imply that all Quakers everywhere have pushed the frontiers of social justice—far from it—but that many seek, in the Quaker phrase, to live up to the light they are given.

Friends in the twenty-first century live in many nations and cultures, but most still believe that faith is meaningless without visible consequences in how their lives are led. They hold a vision of the beloved community molded by the teachings of Christ. They are called to work to better the lives of those who suffer in poverty, to seek to eliminate the causes of war, and to counter the broader culture's emphasis on amassing wealth by living simply. Their ideal is to seek the divine spark in every person and to speak with honesty and integrity.

BOX 1.1   THE KINGDOM OF GOD IS COME AND COMING

Friends use many names to identify the source of truth and power that they know within: the Inward Light, the True Guide, the Pure Principle, and many more. This holy guiding Spirit, they find, not only shows them when they have fallen short of compassion and the way of justice, but also points the way to live in accord with the kingdom of God—a kingdom to be realized here and now on earth rather than through apocalyptic change in some distant future. This is the power that George Fox came to know when he encountered "the one who can speak to my condition." This Spirit changed him inwardly and he came to trust its guidance in daily actions even when its leadings seemed difficult or perhaps even incomprehensible. Quakers continue to believe that this day-to-day awareness and worshipful listening for guidance by individuals and the community makes God visible in the world in each generation.

PEACEMAKING

Friends are perhaps best known for their refusal to participate in war and their efforts to replace warmaking with peacemaking. They asserted early on that war is not the way of Christ. Although many Friends still refuse to participate in the military as conscientious objectors to war, this witness been expanded to prioritize peace-building and prevention of violence at the personal as well as the national level. Readers might recognize Quaker work to relieve wartime suffering resulting from twentieth-century wars from Europe to Vietnam. However, we want to start with a twenty-first-century example from Kenya.

Kenya has long been considered one of the most stable countries in Africa, but widespread violence followed the national elections in 2007. Over a thousand Kenyans died from political violence in the first two months of 2008. Six hundred thousand internally displaced persons had to search for shelter after being forced from their homes. Friends immediately began to find food for the internal refugees. They supported peace teams, provided funds to restore water and electricity, met with youth involved in the violence, and took steps to reduce the tensions between Kikuyu and Kalenjin tribes among other efforts to restore just and peaceful relations. Friends Church Kenya wrote to Mwai Kibaki and Raila Odinga, the two major presidential candidates. Their letter outlined actions Friends were taking for trauma healing and teaching people through the Alternatives to Violence Project (AVP) and other approaches to personal change and ended with a call for others to join in this work.

A crucial dimension of this peace work has been active listening, by both the facilitators and participants in workshops. Recognition of the humanity of those who do violence allows all present to truly hear what is needed to rebuild their communities. Initially this work focused on personal healing and reconciliation. Peace educator Cornelius Ambiah was involved in this work from the start. He spoke about visiting the camps for internally displaced people:

> When we went there we had some food stuffs, but what stood out for me ... [was] to give them emotional support ... so they don't lose hope. To make them feel like they are still wanted, they are still

human beings, that the kind of environment that they were living in is not an obstacle for them to still be strong and able to see whatever are their desires in life

(Lumb 2012, p. 66)

Reconciliation work has continued, especially in Western Kenya where the majority of Friends live and where much of the election violence was centered. Friends have helped people recover from trauma, forgive neighbors, and find ways to restore trust. During subsequent elections they focused on stopping rumors. This task was greatly helped by spread of cell phones that allowed rapid confirmation or contradiction of reports of violence or damage. Sustaining trust was an essential element; word spread that Friends could be trusted not to favor one party or another. Turning The Tide is another important program that engages Kenyans in challenging injustice and pressing for accountability. As these Friends worked, they also did much to train facilitators so that peace work could spread as widely as possible, including establishment of a peace curriculum in schools.

INTEGRITY AND WHOLENESS

Adam Curle, a British Friend, served as a mediator during the Nigerian Civil War of 1967–1970. He quickly became aware that it was essential to develop trust and to engage the leaders of the factions without fear. He writes:

I became aware that what my friends and I were saying was often not heard, especially at the start of a meeting or if the situation were particularly tense. A question or observation would, it is true, be answered, but not responded to in any meaningful way. It was as though our words were filtered through a compound of anger, fear, resentment and preconception that radically changed their meaning.

(1981, p. 58)

He reports on a meeting at the headquarters of a guerilla leader at the height of the hostilities. Prior to the meeting, he spent time listening within himself and letting go of fears that would build distrust. The leader was initially wary and cold, but suddenly smiled, commenting "people don't usually come to see me looking happy and relaxed" (1981, p. 62). The two men became friends and were able to begin to resolve dangerous issues as they relied on that deeper truth of their common humanity.

When Friends speak of "truth" they are pointing to the need for honesty and integrity in their lives so that actions are consistent with professed beliefs. For example, one does not condemn violence in one situation and condone it in another. From the earliest days, they took seriously Jesus' admonition to "Swear not at all." They understood these words as a call to reject a double standard between honesty in everyday interactions and honesty compelled by oath. Quaker merchants gained the reputation for charging a fixed and honest price.

Friends believed that truth-telling in daily life is grounded in the larger Truth they know from the Inward Christ, a Truth that requires honesty about their own inward state and faith in the transformation of oneself in the Light. This knowledge is based in attentive listening for the guidance of the Spirit, clarity about individual prejudices and behavior, and obedience to the divine voice within. Living in this larger truth can heal hearts and bring people into wholeness in their sense of self and open their heart to actions formed in compassion and justice.

Alternatives to Violence Project (AVP) had its roots in the deadly violence at Attica Prison in upstate New York in 1971. After the massacre of Attica prisoners, inmates at New York's Green Haven Prison approached members of a Quaker Project on Community Conflict for help in developing ways to prevent the spread of violence. Quakers and inmates worked together to craft a series of workshops for teaching the skills of nonviolence, particularly to young prisoners. Run by volunteers, AVP was active in roughly 50 countries by 2020. It tries to help people find ways to trust their neighbors and engage with each other in their communities, not only in the midst of tense political situations or in the aftermath of massive killings but also in the face of everyday, personal conflict such as schoolyard bullying. An AVP workshop facilitator offered this description:

AVP workshops are grounded in honesty, respect for others and learning to trust one's own capacity to engage in the world in a way that does not rely on violence, anger and hatred. AVP is about people from all different backgrounds coming together to be in community. When I see participants making themselves vulnerable by sharing and being open to change, I am inspired to manage my own conflict better. We are all transformed, and that transformation ripples outward throughout our communities.

AVP remains an important program in prisons, but its expansive value has become evident in the aftermath of war and genocide. AVP is an important dimension of the Quaker-led African Great Lakes Initiative in Rwanda, Burundi, and the Congo, nations that have been wracked by civil war and genocidal conflict between ethnic groups. In these countries, where people may find themselves living near to people who killed their family, AVP has paired with Quaker-based HROC (Healing and Rebuilding Our Communities). The result is an important tool for people to rebuild communities where trauma has torn apart trust among villagers. The programs also offer prisoners a new way to interact both on the "inside" and as they return to their homes on the "outside." David Niyonzima, a Quaker pastor who narrowly escaped death in the genocide, organized THARS (Trauma Healing and Reconciliation Services) in 2000, while Burundi's 12-year civil war was still raging. The initial programs were reconciliation workshops between Hutu and Tutsi who had been pitted against each other in the war. An important aspect of THARS work was to train over 2,000 individuals in this work and to set up safe listening centers for those who had been traumatized.

YOUR SONS *AND* YOUR DAUGHTERS SHALL PROPHESY (ACTS 2:17)

In 1957, the Copajira Bible School in Bolivia, founded by Quaker missionaries, began to offer instruction for 73 young Aymara women who were then sent out to give testimony to the work of Christ in their lives. The response was sometimes hostile. People pelted some of these young women with sticks and stones and set dogs on them. Nonetheless, these women carried on. They were among the first literate Aymara women and helped to break down the marginalization of women. Missionaries Jack and Geraldine Willcuts further broke down the gender barriers as Jack at times took on traditional women's chores such as ironing while Geraldine took the lead of teaching. This commitment to opening opportunities for women is an active part of Quaker mission work and the growth of Quaker faith and practice in the twenty-first century.

From the earliest days Friends acted on the words of the biblical prophet Joel, repeated in Acts 2, that your "sons and daughters" shall prophesy. Early Quaker convert Margaret Fell drew on biblical texts in her powerful pamphlet "Womens Speaking Justified" (see Chapter 2). The Bolivian example has parallels elsewhere. Kenyan Rasoah Mutuha had a clear call to ministry in the 1920s and encouraged women to be like Deborah, the judge of the Israelites, and be faithful to battle for God. In this she was a voice for resistance to both colonialism and patriarchal norms. Nepal is a newer example where the Quaker welcoming of women's ministry and value to the community stands out not only in contrast to the local culture but also to other Christian denominations.

While Friends like to celebrate their stance on equality for all people and recognize that the Holy Spirit is available in every heart, practices have been uneven. Quakers did not accept African Americans into membership until the late eighteenth century and women were not full partners in conducting the business of Quaker meetings until the mid-nineteenth or, in some places, the twentieth century. There remains wide disagreement among Quakers worldwide about equality for gay, lesbian, and transgender people. North American yearly meetings have separated over this issue, and meetings in the Global South generally classify homosexual behavior as a sin. European Friends almost unanimously advocate for full equality, and Friends in the United States are divided.[1] This lack of agreement parallels similar Protestant denominations such as the United Methodist Church and the Anglican Communion.

CARE FOR THE LEAST OF THESE

In 1947, Margaret Backhouse of Friends Service Committee (FSC) of Britain and Henry Cadbury of the American Friends Service Committee (AFSC) accepted the Nobel Peace Prize on behalf of all Friends. The Prize recognized years of relief work in the aftermath of war, particularly World War II, but also following previous conflicts. Friends were adamant that politics would not dictate who got food and who didn't, and focused particularly on children. There are other examples of Quaker concern for the powerless from the same years of global war. In 1938 Quakers helped organize the Kindertransport that allowed 10,000 Jewish children to leave Germany, and welcomed them into their families for the duration of the war. In the United States, Quakers sought to ameliorate the forced removal of Japanese Americans to internment camps in 1942 under the pressure of wartime fears. In his presentation speech, Gunnar Jahn, chair of the Nobel Committee, recounted examples of Quaker relief work, pointing out that it was not the extent of this work, but the spirit in which it was performed that was so important:

> The Quakers have shown us that it is possible to carry into action something which is deeply rooted in the minds of many: sympathy with others; the desire to help others ... without regard to nationality or race; feelings which, when carried into deeds, must provide the foundations of a lasting peace. For this reason, they are today worthy of receiving Nobel's Peace Prize.

This care for others continues in many forms. The plight of the Iraqi civilians who were innocent victims of the United States invasion of 2003 deeply moved Noah Baker Merrill, a young New England Friend. In 2007, he worked in Iraq as co-founder of Direct Aid Iraq, which brought together Iraqis and Americans in an organization advocating for American responsibility to support a peaceful future for Iraqis. They worked together to build personal relationships as part of that restitution process. They linked to a global network connecting Iraqis with urgent medical care on a case-by-case basis, advocated for resettlement of displaced people, and facilitated others doing similar work. He described one of his interactions:

> We'd been visiting Umm Luay, the mother of three daughters, who worked in a chemical weapons factory in Iraq until a U.S. airstrike came. Because of the chemicals to which she was exposed in the aftermath, all three of her beautiful young daughters are wheelchair-bound ... Direct

> Aid Iraq [provided] the family ... pastoral care, physical therapy, medicine, and support advocating with other aid providers in Amman.

Merrill and others found themselves blessed by the family's humor, their guidance about was needed, and their help in identifying others in need. The task of aiding seriously injured Iraqis transformed the American as well, drawing him into a ministry for peace and justice as well as supporting others in such work.

Peace work in war-ravaged nations like Iraq has dangers as well as rewards. A number of Friends have committed themselves to help others in some of the most troubled parts of the world, working with either Christian Peacemakers Teams or Friends Peace Teams. Tom Fox, a Virginia Quaker, had a strong leading to aid Iraqi citizens harmed by the US invasion of their country. He joined with other Christian Peacemakers to defend the human rights of Iraqis caught in the turmoil. His call to service echoed that of early Friends as he sought to bring the weapons of the Spirit into the front lines of conflict. In 2005 a splinter group of militants kidnapped Fox and three other Christian Peacemakers workers and held them hostage for several months. The others were freed by military action but Tom Fox was found murdered, a reminder that answering the call of God can be as dangerous in the twenty-first century as it was for very early Quakers.

CARE FOR THE EARTH: WHAT IS ENOUGH?

Many Friends know that the Earth is in crisis in the twenty-first century. They are increasingly aware of the long-term implications of choices about the share of its resources that we each claim. Aspects of this have long been visible in such testimonies as simplicity and plain dress. Such witness against the accumulation of wealth and power echoes the Epistle of James, chapter 4, which directly addresses the causes of war. While there were early Friends who took what we would now call environmental stands such as vegetarianism and battling cruelty to animals, the need to care for the natural environment emerged as a prominent issue as part of the broader environmental movement of the later twentieth and twenty-first centuries.

In 2018, British Friend Jocelyn Bell Burnell received a Special Breakthrough Prize in Fundamental Physics. The $3 million award recognized her major accomplishments in astronomy. An astrophysicist, she co-discovered the first radio pulsars in 1967, a discovery which has been called one of the most significant scientific achievements of the twentieth century. However, she has had to battle sex-based discrimination throughout her career and was not named as a co-recipient of the 1974 Nobel Prize in Physics, despite the fact that she was the first to observe pulsars. While she cherished the honor of the Breakthrough Prize, she gave away the financial award. Her decision to give her new wealth to fund students from groups underrepresented in physics was an act of humility and concern for the whole of society very much in keeping with her faith, an example of rejecting the temptations of overconsumption are part of caring for the earth.

The awareness of the responsibility to find our rightful place in the world for the sake of humanity and the planet is evident in the decisions that many individual Quakers and organizations make on a regular basis. In 2005, the Friends Committee on National Legislation (FCNL) rebuilt its Civil War era headquarters building in Washington, DC. FCNL offices became the first LEED certified green building on Capitol Hill. It has welcomed visiting members of Congress, the Architect of the Capitol, and many others who are in a position to encourage federal government construction to embody environmentally sensitive features. Aside from the many tours conducted in the building, senators also mentioned how often they would take visitors to the roof of the adjacent Hart Senate Office Building to look down onto the FCNL building's green roof, something relatively common now, but a novelty at the start of the twenty-first century.

Philadelphia Quaker writer and activist Eileen Flanagan served as clerk of the board of Earth Quaker Action Team (EQAT) while it confronted PNC Bank over its environmental impact. The bank is a Philadelphia institution that claims both Quaker roots and a green ethic. EQAT challenged it to live up to its words by ending its financing of mountaintop coal mining in Appalachia. They did not want to destroy the bank, but rather hoped to strengthen a real commitment to protection of the environment. Often EQAT used tactics that surprised others and pricked consciences. For example, members sang "Where Have All the Flowers Gone?" in front of the PNC pavilion at the 2011 Philadelphia Flower Show and "Which Side Are You On?" to each member of the PNC board during their 2013 shareholder meeting. Combining these tactics with more traditional organizing and actions at dozens of PNC branches, EQAT was successful in changing the behavior of a major institution. EQAT draws its strength from bringing spirituality into its action and draws in many individuals who, as Eileen says, "have experienced a powerful connection to the Divine in action." It is not hard to transport the spirit of unprogrammed worship to corporate board rooms.

WELCOMING THE STRANGER

Jim Corbett's faith led him from the American Southwest to Central America to accompany refugees from violence in Guatemala and El Salvador. Corbett, a key figure in the immigrant sanctuary movement of the 1980s, titled his memoir *Goatwalking* because he had spent many years with herds of goats in the Arizona mountains. This practice built the skills he used to escort refugees to sanctuary churches in the United States. His direct social action benefited from this work and his extensive knowledge of the Sonoran Desert. He was at home in the desert, knowing how to live off the land as he guided people through what has been called a modern incarnation of the underground railroad. He made no attempt to hide his identity as he became involved with other church leaders in the region, visiting immigrants in Mexico and doing what he could to help people reach sanctuary further north. He suggests that the key is to act with humility and always be open to positive interaction even with corrupt officials—a very practical application of seeing God in everyone. Here is how he described finding a path to live out his faith: "Goatwalking opened the way for me to read the Bible in the present, as covenanting in which I, as much as Joshua and Paul, am a participant. Learning to read the Bible in the present is the key to participation in the prophetic faith" (1991, p. 4).

Friends' concern for would-be immigrants was and is part of Quaker concern for people who are dispossessed. In India, for instance, much Quaker mission work has been among the Chamar caste, a group of socially scorned leatherworkers of Bundelkhand. In Bolivia, they reached out to the Aymara people. While Friends in the Global North are divided on immigration issues, several meetings have given sanctuary to immigrants fleeing danger in Central America. Three young immigration lawyers who worship with us in our own Quaker meeting are among the many who continue to fight for the rights of others to find asylum and safety in the United States despite increasingly strict limits on entry.

EVERYDAY PROPHETS

In 2016, three Australian grandmothers donned quaint Quaker bonnets and set up a table beside the gate to the secretive Pine Gap military base, which helps to coordinate US drone strikes. They laid out croissants and tea on a white tablecloth and engaged workers in conversation when they arrived for their morning shift. The previous year they paid $500 fines after setting up in front of the gate to another Australian base, again successfully raising awareness of Australia's cooperation with the US military.

In 1973, after a tornado destroyed much of the town of Xenia, Ohio, members of several local Friends churches came together to help. The result was Friends Disaster Service, a network of volunteers from Quaker churches around the United States who have come together to help repair ravaged communities in the US and other nations. Their volunteers often go where large relief organizations do not, such as small towns outside New Orleans that were also devastated by Hurricane Katrina in 2005.

Most Quakers are neither as imaginative nor as determined as the "Quaker grannies" (nor, we can say, as much fun to know). Nor are they able to drop what they are doing to bring help to people thousands of miles away like Friends Disaster Service volunteers. We've used this chapter to highlight stories of Quakers "living up to their light" to use a Quaker term for drawing on spiritual resources to walk their talk. Like members of any group, few Friends are pioneers and saints. Few twenty-first-century Quakers are a Jim Corbett or a David Niyonzima, just as few earlier Quakers were another John Woolman or Lucretia Mott. Then and now, most take smaller and more cautious steps while trying to live up to their ideals.

We see these steps in our own meeting, which includes both the immigration attorneys and those who support them in practical ways. One couple regularly travels to Guatemala to support a Quaker-based program that has helped to provide higher education opportunities for 1500 indigenous students since 1973. One has worked to organize advocacy for progressive issues in the Oregon legislature. Another has a ministry of music that lifts up concern for the natural environment as a spiritual calling, bringing that message into the very secular world of clubs and bars. Still others are working to reform a biased criminal justice system and promote restorative justice. Along with other Friends meetings and churches in the Portland area, we support Quaker Voluntary Service, which offers young adults an opportunity to work with peace, community development, and social change organizations. None of these efforts is headline news, but all of them are small steps toward the more just and peaceful world that early Friends envisioned.

Although the mundane details of Quaker work for peace and justice often look very much like the similar work by secular political and social action groups, the difference is acting from a place of faith as everyday prophets, seeking divine guidance. In the next chapters we explore the evolution of the Quaker beliefs that underlie their public roles, describe the institutions and practices that they have developed since the seventeenth century, and describe the Quaker presence around the world.

NOTE

1   Yearly meetings are regional or national association of local meetings and churches, so named because they traditionally met once a year to conduct business.

FURTHER READING

Adam Curle, *True Justice: Quaker Peace Makers and Peace Making* (London: Quaker Home Service, 1981). A pioneer in the field of Peace Studies presents a faith-based Quaker approach to resolving conflicts.

Brian Drayton, *On Living with a Concern for the Gospel Ministry* (Philadelphia: Quaker Press, 2006). An exploration of ways in which Friends are called to be ministers, whether through vocal messages during worship or action in the world.

Lon Fendall, *Citizenship: A Christian Calling* (Newberg, OR: Barclay Press, 2003). An evangelical Friend with experience in Washington, D.C. on ways to approach government as an instrument of compassion and justice.

Esther Mombo and Cécile Nyiramana, *Mending Broken Hearts, Rebuilding Shattered Lives: Quaker Peacebuilding in East and Central Africa* (London: Quaker Books, 2016). Kenyan and Rwandan Quakers on peace and reconciliation work Kenya and neighboring countries.

William Taber, *The Prophetic Stream* (Wallingford, PA: Pendle Hill Publications, 1984). A compact and powerful booklet that its publisher accurately describes as a shout-out to revive the prophetic message in Quaker worship and ministry and in Christianity.

A DANGER TO THE NATION
THE FIRST GENERATIONS OF QUAKERISM IN THE SEVENTEENTH CENTURY

> The said persons, under a pretence of religious worship, do often assemble themselves in great numbers in several parts of this realm, to the great endangering of the public peace and safety, and to the terror of the people, by maintaining a secret and strict correspondence among themselves, and in the meantime separating and dividing themselves from the rest of his majesty's good and loyal subjects, and from the public congregations and usual places of divine worship.
>
> (Quaker Act, passed by Parliament in 1661 and in effect in 1662)

Near the Massachusetts Statehouse in Boston is a statue of the Quaker Mary Dyer, depicted as middle-aged woman in plain colonial garb, seated quietly with a sober and serene expression. English Puritans had established and settled Massachusetts in the 1630s as an ideal Christian commonwealth that could set an example for reform of the English church. The colony's governing institutions were open only to church members, making it effectively a theocracy where religious and political dissent were entangled. Mary Dyer challenged the Massachusetts church authorities and paid with her life.

Mary Dyer emigrated to Massachusetts from England in 1635 and got into trouble three years later, while in her early twenties. In 1638 the Massachusetts authorities banished her to the somewhat more tolerant Rhode Island colony for taking the losing side in a Puritan theological dispute. Going back to England in 1652, she became an early convert to the radical new teachings of George Fox, the founder of the Religious Society of Friends. Back in New England a few years later, she found that Massachusetts had outlawed Quaker practice and preaching for undermining both religious and civil authority. Nevertheless, she traveled to Boston to preach and to challenge these restrictions. She was expelled, came back, and was banished. She returned a third time and was sentenced to death along with two Quaker men but given a last-minute reprieve and forcibly removed from the colony (the men were not spared). Dyer refused to remain free when other Quakers in Massachusetts faced death. She returned yet a fourth time in 1660, when the sentence of death by hanging was carried out. Her last words reiterated her fundamental opposition to the Massachusetts law: "I came to keep blood guiltiness from you, desiring you to repeal the unrighteous and unjust law made against the innocent servants of the Lord." Hers is a story of radical belief, stubborn action, and martyrdom. It also shows how dangerous early Quakers seemed to government leaders who saw an official church as a bulwark of public order.

This chapter traces the Quaker movement from its beginnings with a former shoemaker's apprentice, George Fox, to its successful establishment in North America with the work of the well-connected and highly respectable William Penn. The first section describes the initial vision of George Fox and the explosive growth of a Quaker movement. The second details the faith and beliefs of very early Quakers that set them apart from other religious radicals in England, and the third section outlines early efforts to turn a passionate but inchoate movement into a stable and lasting religious society. The last section brings Quakers from Britain to English colonies in the Caribbean islands and the mainland of North America. Over the course of the chapter, we show how Quakers came to be seen as a threat to public order, how they struggled to allay the fears of the government while remaining true to their beliefs, and how they eventually managed to flourish in seventeenth-century England and spread successfully to Jamaica, Barbados, Rhode Island, New Jersey, Pennsylvania, and the Carolinas.

GEORGE FOX AND QUAKER FOUNDATIONS

In 1640s, teenaged George Fox left home in the midst of the raging English Civil War between adherents of Charles I and

Table 2.1 Early Quakers in the context of seventeenth-century England

	Society of Friends	English History
1620s	1624: George Fox born	1625: Charles I becomes king
1630s		1629–40: Charles I rules without Parliament
1640s	1647: George Fox's conversion experience	1642–8: Parliament defeats royalists in Civil War 1647–9: Levellers agitate for radical democracy 1649: Charles I executed
1650s	1652: George Fox's vision on Pendle Hill and sermon on Firbank Fell begin Quaker movement 1656: James Nayler convicted of blasphemy	1653–8: Oliver Cromwell rules as Lord Protector
1660s	1662: Quaker worship outlawed 1669: Margaret Fell marries George Fox	1660: Restoration of monarchy with Charles II 1661–5: Anti-Quaker laws 1666: Great Fire ravages London
1670s	1670: Trial of William Penn and William Meade establishes independence of juries 1671–3: George Fox travels and preaches in the New World 1671–5: British Quakers establish national coordinating committees such as Meeting for Sufferings 1675: Quakers settle in New Jersey 1676: Robert Barclay's *Apology* grounds Quakerism in Christian theology	1673: Test Act excludes Catholics and dissenting Protestants from public office
1680s	1681: William Penn obtains charter for Pennsylvania	1685: James II becomes king 1688: Glorious Revolution replaces Catholic James II with Mary II and her husband William III. 1689: Toleration Act extends freedom of worship to dissenting Protestants
1690s	1691: George Fox dies 1694: *Journal of George Fox* published	

supporters of an independent Parliament. A wide variety of new groups and sects saw the end of the monarchy as a chance for economic reform and the more perfect realization of the kingdom of God on earth. There were Seekers, Levellers, Muggletonians, Ranters, and Diggers, creating more uproar at a time when Oliver Cromwell was trying to gain control of England and restore economic and political stability. The Civil War ended with the execution of Charles in 1649 and left the most radical groups briefly hopeful for fundamental social change.

George Fox was distressed at the emptiness of church ritual and found written treatises wanting. Christians whose actions did not match their professed beliefs left him deeply frustrated. He was also estranged from his conventional parents. In the depths of despair in 1647 he heard a disembodied voice proclaiming, "There is one, even Christ Jesus, who can speak to thy condition." He felt his heart leap for joy at these words and soon was preaching across the countryside about the direct reality and guidance of the living Christ. In 1650 he entered a steeple house (as he called all church buildings, asserting that people are the church). Upon hearing the priest declare the Scriptures as central, he reported in his journal: "Now the Lord's power was so mighty upon me, and so strong in me, that I could not hold, but was made to cry out and say, 'Oh no, it is not the Scriptures,' and was commanded to tell them that God did not dwell in temples made with hands" (quoted in Moore 2000, p. 10). Fox was arrested as a disruptive influence and imprisoned for nearly a year.

Fox was 28 years old when his 1652 vision on Pendle Hill of a "great people to be gathered" inspired him to preach and gather followers. The gathering that followed at Firbank Fell was the start of something big. Fox was soon at the center of a growing number of seekers, veterans of the Civil War who were disillusioned with Oliver Cromwell, and others who worshipped separately from the Church of England. The new movement grew explosively with missionary zeal. Traveling ministers dubbed the "Valiant Sixty" spread the message to southern England, working in pairs of two men or two women, at a time when women were considered by some to have no more soul than a goose. Quaker missionaries were soon traveling to Northern Europe, to the Mediterranean, and across the Atlantic. They were a movement energized by their vision of God's truth and its accessibility to all. George Fox himself traveled to Ireland, the Netherlands, Barbados and Jamaica in the Caribbean, and the English colonies in North America.

Many voices spoke for the new movement along with Fox and the Valiant Sixty. James Nayler, who sometimes traveled with Fox, was considered by many to be Fox's equal as a spiritual leader and guide. In 1656, however, while Fox was again in prison, Nayler listened to followers who had the very bad idea that he ride into the city of Bristol in a reenactment of the entry of Jesus into Jerusalem. The intent was to symbolize that God was as much present in the immediate moment as in Bible times. The authorities thought differently, arresting him and convicting him of blasphemy. Other Quakers disowned him, and the nascent Society of Friends worried about its reputation and survival (the Boston officials who struggled to deal with Mary Dyer would likely have known about Nayler and the disruptive reputation of English Quakers). Fox reluctantly reconciled with Nayler when he was released from prison in 1659. The next year Nayler was mugged and left for dead by the roadside; his last recorded words begin "there is a spirit which I feel that delights to do no evil, not to revenge any wrong, but delights to endure all things."

BOX 2.1   THE LAMB'S WAR

The most radical Friends sometimes drew on biblical imagery of Christ as the Lamb of God as described in Revelation. They saw themselves engaged in the Lamb's War against the forces of darkness, a war fought not with physical weapons but as a spiritual, nonviolent contest against their own sinfulness and the outward evils of established church and clergy. George Fox preached about the Lamb's War in the mid-1650s but muted the concept in later years, particularly because its most articulate proponent had been the problematic James Nayler. Nayler described this conflict as "not against creatures, not with flesh and blood, but spiritual wickedness ... against the whole Work and Device of the god of this World, Laws, Customs, fashions, Inventions, this is all Enmity against the Lamb and his followers."

(Nayler, *The Lambs Warre*, 1657)

In response to the Bristol debacle, more cautious Quakers tried to maintain their unorthodox approach to Christianity while keeping a lower profile. In October 1656, a conference of northern Quakers issued what is known as the Epistle of the Elders of Balby (a small town in Yorkshire). Along with advice on how to keep local groups functioning smoothly, they included the admonition "that if any be called to serve the commonwealth in any public service, which is for the public wealth and good, that with cheerfulness it be undertaken, and in faithfulness discharged." In other words, do your civic duty as best you can unless it directly violates your religious convictions. In 1661, after restoration of the monarchy with Charles II, George Fox and other Quaker leaders wrote the king that "we utterly deny all outward wars and strife and fightings with outward weapons, or any end or under any pretense whatsoever." The statement, which has served as the foundation of the modern Quaker peace testimony, had the practical purpose of telling the government that Quakers had no intention of getting involved in any armed resistance to the restored monarchy.

Despite these sorts of assurances, Quakers remained at a severe legal disadvantage. The ban on Quakers in Massachusetts anticipated one of the first actions of the English Parliament after the restoration of the monarchy. The "Quaker Act," whose preamble opens this chapter, went into effect in 1662—only ten years after the movement's beginnings. It aimed to prevent "the mischiefs and dangers that may arise by certaine persons called Quakers and others, refusing to take lawful oaths," meaning in particular an oath of allegiance to the Crown. The problem was that Quakers refused to swear oaths on theological grounds based on their literal reading of the Bible. The law also forbade assembly in any pretense of worship by Quakers over age 16. Strict enforcement of this and other laws aimed generally at Dissenters led to massive imprisonment. An estimated 15,000 Friends suffered imprisonment for worshipping outside the church and refusing to take oaths or to pay tithes to support the clergy, and more than 400 died from filth and disease.[1]

THE MIGHTY POWER OF THE LORD: EARLY QUAKER BELIEFS

Friends, despite their modern association with silent worship, were not always quiet. Some Friends did meet in quietness, but open meetings aimed at newcomers were often marked by spontaneous sermons lasting an hour or more. Even more notorious were their group experiences of trembling or quaking during worship. Robert Barclay, the primary Quaker theologian, wrote that "sometimes the Power of God will break forth into a whole meeting ... and thereby trembling ... will be upon most ... which as the power of truth prevails, will from pangs and groans end with the sweet sound of thanksgiving and praise" (Barbour 1964, p. 36). The popular name "Quakers," which early Friends initially disliked, was apparently first used by a judge sentencing George Fox. Friends often named themselves "those in scorn called Quakers" on the title page of their literature to make clear their early disdain for the term.

Early "Quakers" adopted a very different terminology to name and characterize their movement. William Penn, in his introduction to George Fox's *Journal* (1952, p. xxxv), wrote that Fox said that "his authority was inward and not outward, and that he got it and kept it by the love of God and power of an endless life." A series of strong visions and openings defined his faith in the Light of Christ, available to all men, women and children, which formed the basis of Quaker faith and practice. Seeking to name what made their movement distinctive, they initially used names such as "Children of the Light." They settled on "Friends of Truth" and ultimately simply "Friends," referring to the Gospel of John (15:12–17):

> This is my commandment, that you love one another as I have loved you. No one has greater love than this, to lay down one's life for one's friends. You are my friends if you do what I command you. I do not call you servants any longer, because a servant does not know what the master is doing; but I have called you friends, because I have made know to you everything that I have heard from my Father. You did not choose me but I chose you. And I appointed you to go and bear fruit, fruit that will last, so that the Father will give you whatever you ask him in my name. I am giving you these commandments so that you may love one another.

The ground of their faith was direct experience of God, or the Light of Christ within, which was strong enough to shake people to their cores—and yes, sometimes cause them to tremble and quake outwardly. They knew with certainty that Christ was to be found in this experience, not in the pages of a book, even the Bible, and not dependent on the words of priests. The Light of Christ is available to all people, if they will only attend to it. It will show each person their sins—"the eternal light … will rip you up" in the words of Margaret Fell—but then it will point out the way forward. Each person had the responsibility to listen to the Voice of the Light (Christ's voice) in their deepest consciousness, and obey it.

Friends often named one another as prophets, individuals who spoke words given by God, and they sought to live out the kingdom of God on earth. They were deeply familiar with the Bible as a source of divine guidance (Michael Birkel has pointed out that George Fox could pack seven different biblical references into a single paragraph). At the same time, they might choose to go out into a field and listen quietly before taking action. They rejected statements of belief that did not become visible in the way people lived. They saw their faith as helping to realize God's kingdom now, on earth, as well as in heaven. For theological justification, they cited the Gospel of Luke (17:21): "Once Jesus was asked by the Pharisees when the kingdom of God was coming, and he answered, The kingdom of God is not coming with things that can be observed; nor will they say, 'Look, here it is!' or 'There it is!' For, in fact the kingdom of God is among you."

BOX 2.2 SPIRITUAL ADVICE FOR FRIENDS

Early Friends believed that opening themselves to God invited deep personal insight and led to radical spiritual transformation as they tried to live in accord with that new understanding. An early statement came in Margaret Fell's *Epistle to Convinced Friends* from 1656:

Friends, deal plainly with yourselves, and let the eternal light search you, and try you, for the good of your souls; for this will deal plainly with you; it will rip you up, lay you open, and make all manifest that lodgeth in you; the secret subtlety of the enemy of your souls, this searcher and tryer will make manifest … consider one another, and provoke one another to love and to good works; not forsaking the assembling of yourselves, but exhorting one another, and so much the more, as you see the day approaching. And dwell in love and unity, in the pure eternal light; there is your fellowship, there is your cleansing and washing ... And the ever-lasting God, of light, life and power, keep you all faithful to your own measure; that so the resurrection and the life ye may witness, and the living bread ye may feed on, which, whosoever eateth of, shall never die.

One of the foundations of the Protestant Reformation had been the translation of the Bible from Latin into the languages that ordinary people spoke and possibly read. What we can call "Bible politics" revolved around who was privileged to interpret the Bible and how absolute was its authority. Friends' conviction that Christ is always present in each soul meant that they rejected the need for priests and saw the Bible as a secondary source of truth. Friends were thus on one extreme of rancorous debates. There was also some ambiguity, in that Fox is said to have known the Bible so thoroughly that he could have reproduced it should it disappear. Biblical language permeated his preaching and writing, and early Quaker theologians Robert Barclay and Elizabeth Bathurst both drew heavily on Bible passages to legitimate Quaker beliefs. In general, Friends struck a balance by arguing that the Spirit would not lead to action contrary to Scripture when it was read with divine guidance.

Friends understood the sacraments as inward and spiritual, decrying the outward forms when no inward transformation accompanied the baptismal water or the consumption of the communion bread and wine. They asserted that people too often battled over the external rituals without grasping the powerful life of their spiritual essence. Ephesians 4:5 names the "one baptism which is the baptism by the Spirit" and which purifies the soul. Friends therefore declared that the inward and spiritual nature of the sacraments removed the need for water baptism, ordained clergy, and other forms so central to the Church of England. These and other distinctive aspects of their theology shaped their practice even as it upset and sometimes enraged church and government officials.

Quakers also opposed adherence to a creed as a way to measure spiritual vitality and authenticity, instead emphasizing the individual's relationship with the divine. They believed that they were reviving and restoring original Christian practice from its first centuries, an idea that William Penn summarized in *Primitive Christianity Revived* (1696), where "primitive" meant early or original.

Again and again they referred to the Gospel of John, particularly to the prologue with its stress on Light, Word, and Spirit. However, they did not accept the common Protestant identification of the Word of God with the words of the Bible. Instead, they asserted that Christ present among all people *was* the Word. They paid little attention to the historical Jesus and ignored doctrines such as the virgin birth. They believed that the reason to read the Scriptures was to be drawn toward the Light, and that salvation was universally available for all people including those who never heard of Jesus. In Elizabeth Bathurst's words:

> Thus I have again toucht upon the former Particulars, wherein I undertook to Vindicate Truth and its Followers, in all which Christ (the Light and Life of Man) is all in all unto his People: for Christianity doth not consist in the belief in so many Doctrines, Articles and Principles (as some suppose) but in conformity unto that one Eternal Principle, to wit, the Light of Christ manifest in the Conscience ... that one Gift of Light and Grace through Christ Jesus freely bestowed on all Men; and according to the Improvement that they make of their measures, so an increase thereof is administered to them ... And this Word [Christ] that reconcileth, is not afar off; 'tis not in Heaven, that any should say, Who shall go up for us, and bring it down to us, that we may hear it and do it? ... but the Word is very nigh unto thee, in thy Mouth, and in thy Heart, that thou may'st hear it and do it. So then the Indians and Americans shall not perish for want of the Bible, which we have here in England.
>
> (Bathurst quoted in Garman, et al. 1996, pp. 382, 390)

Friends sometimes used the apocalyptic imagery from Revelation, but their main focus was on God's love and desire for salvation for all people. Friends made much use of the first epistle of John and its references to sinlessness in their doctrine of perfection and resultant belief that it is possible to live without sin under Christ's guidance. 1 John 2:5 asserts that "the love of God has reached perfection" in those who obey God. Matthew 5:48 offers the instruction to "be perfect, therefore, as you heavenly Father is perfect." The Greek word translated into English as "perfect" (*teleios*) usually signifies coming into full maturity and wholeness. Biblical usage often refers to perfect love, not a specific list of actions or beliefs. Robert Barclay devoted one of 15 key propositions in his *Apology* to "Perfection" and noted clearly that while a person might be freed from sin, there was still room for growth and a possibility of sinning. Nonetheless, this assertion of sinlessness was one that often caused Friends to be imprisoned for blasphemy. This ideal of perfect love would also be highlighted in the nineteenth century by Methodists, Wesleyans, Church of the Nazarene, Salvation Army and others who engaged with what became known as the Holiness Movement.

1655 and 1656, were years of high millenarian expectation about the imminent coming of the kingdom of God. However, historian Rosemary Moore notes that Quakers stood apart from many others in England. Rather than expecting an apocalyptic transformation, they emphasized their distinctive view "that the kingdom of God was already, to an extent, present in themselves, and that the full consummation would be attained by spiritual transformation rather than by either secular politics or a final judgment" (Moore 2000, p. 68). This Quaker belief that the kingdom has actually come was of particular note to non-Friends. The kingdom of God had widely been expected to come *now* given the disastrous drumbeat of war, plague, and fire. Gradually during the 1650s, however, Quakers had realized that the end times foretold in Revelation were not about to happen. Instead, they increasingly adopted a spiritualized understanding of the kingdom involving a tension between the "now" and "not yet"—a posture that theologians describe as a "realized eschatology." Friends would have said that the kingdom is both "come and coming."

We close this section with another Bible passage of great significance to early Friends. Jeremiah 31:31 proclaims God's new covenant, whereby the law is placed within and written on the heart. The promise that each person can know God is the foundation for waiting worship where everyone in the congregation has responsibility to listen for divine guidance without dependence on priests or texts. "Walking in the Light" was one way that

Friends described living in the kingdom in their communities and daily life. Theology and practice were thoroughly intertwined and essential to being Children of the Light. This set them visibly apart from most of the population and at odds with the state-supported church. The many difficulties and punishments they encountered were considered to be part of taking up the cross to human will and desires. In such was the power of God.

LINKING THE COMMUNITY OF FRIENDS: FROM SWARTHMOOR HALL TO LONDON

Margaret Fell (1614–1702) is often referred to as the mother of Quakerism. She lived with her husband Thomas Fell, a prominent judge, and her eight children at Swarthmoor Hall in the northwest of England. Fell and most of her household were convinced by their encounter with George Fox in 1652 while Judge Fell was away. He arrived home to the startling news that his wife and seven daughters now saw themselves as followers of Fox, but was willing to meet with Fox and to accept his family's new beliefs. Judge Fell never openly was a Friend, but is said to have sat in the hall nearby when worship was held at his home, and used his position to protect Friends from persecution.

Margaret Fell wrote 16 books and many pamphlets explaining and defending Friends. Her comfortable economic circumstances allowed her to make Swarthmoor Hall an administrative and communications center for Friends. She exchanged letters with Friends traveling in the ministry. Especially in the early years before the center of Quakerism shifted to London, Fell noted where visits were needed, negotiated the release of jailed and persecuted Friends, and administered funds that provided much needed financial stability. She advocated for the creation of the organizational structure of regular meetings for business including the creation of women's meetings. After the death of her husband in 1658 she was twice imprisoned and her estates forfeited for her refusal to take an oath of allegiance to the king. She vigorously defended herself, declaring, "Although I am out of the King's protection, yet I am not out of the protection of almighty God." Eventually she was freed, regained her property, and married George Fox in 1669 (in twenty-first-century language they were a power couple, Quaker style).

BOX 2.3   WOMEN AS MINISTERS

Margaret Fell's position and influence did not mean that all Friends accepted women as full equals. Women were accepted into the ministry and often travelled widely. Some monthly meetings had separate women's business meetings that had limited responsibilities. But women did address some matters of substance and gained experience in public speaking, writing epistles, and persuading men to take action. American women had their own yearly meetings by the mid-1700s and British Friends in 1784. However, nearly another century passed before they had full and equal participation in addressing the business of the community. As with other steps that early Quakers took, what seems limited and unequal from a twenty-first-century viewpoint was unsettling and empowering in the seventeenth century.

Margaret Fell was herself an influential advocate for the recognition of women in the ministry. Her 1666 pamphlet *Womens Speaking Justified, Proved and Allowed of by the Scriptures* was a powerful argument for the spiritual gifts of women that drew on the Gospels, particularly the passage in both Matthew and John in which the risen Christ appears first to women and tells them to spread the good news.

> Those that speak against the power of the Lord, and the Spirit of the Lord speaking in a woman, simply by reason of her sex, or because she is a woman, not regarding the Seed and Spirit and Power that speaks in her, such speak against Christ and his Church ... Jesus owned the love and grace that appeared in women, and did not despise it. And by what is recorded in the Scriptures, he received as much love, kindness, compassion, and tender dealing towards him from women as he did from any others, both in his life-time and also after they had exercised their cruelty upon him ... Mark this, you that despise and oppose the message of the Lord God that he sends by Women. What had become of the redemption of the whole body of mankind, if they had not believed the message that the Lord Jesus sent by these women, of and concerning his resurrection, and so were ready to carry his message.

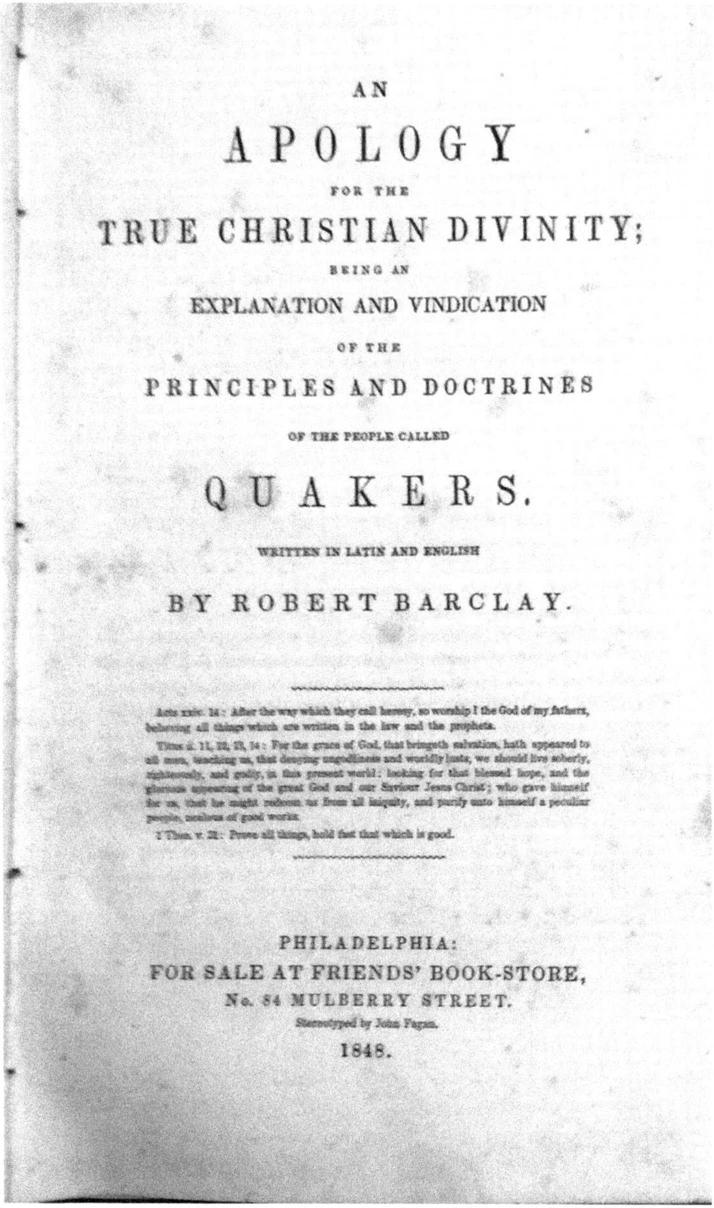

AN

APOLOGY

FOR THE

TRUE CHRISTIAN DIVINITY;

BEING AN

EXPLANATION AND VINDICATION

OF THE

PRINCIPLES AND DOCTRINES

OF THE PEOPLE CALLED

QUAKERS.

WRITTEN IN LATIN AND ENGLISH

BY ROBERT BARCLAY.

Acts xxiv. 14 : After the way which they call heresy, so worship I the God of my fathers, believing all things which are written in the law and the prophets.

Titus ii. 11, 12, 13, 14 : For the grace of God, that bringeth salvation, hath appeared to all men, teaching us, that denying ungodliness and worldly lusts, we should live soberly, righteously, and godly, in this present world : looking for that blessed hope, and the glorious appearing of the great God and our Saviour Jesus Christ ; who gave himself for us, that he might redeem us from all iniquity, and purify unto himself a peculiar people, zealous of good works.

1 Thes. v. 21 : Prove all things, hold fast that which is good.

PHILADELPHIA:

FOR SALE AT FRIENDS' BOOK-STORE,

No. 84 MULBERRY STREET.

Stereotyped by John Fagan.

1848.

Figure 2.1 Barclay's *Apology*: originally published in 1676, Barclay's book justified radical Quakerism as authentically Christian

Most of the dissenting religious groups that arose alongside Friends in the mid-seventeenth century soon faded away. Fell and others worked in the early decades to assure that Friends did not suffer the same decline. They established an orderly structure for conducting the business of the community and maintained a massive correspondence to knit together the far-flung individuals traveling to share their faith. Friends' determination to fully support those in prison and their families was a crucial factor in creating a lasting organization. From early on, each worshipping community of Friends was expected to send to their local monthly meeting responses to queries such as "What ministering Friends have died in the past year?" and "How does Truth prosper among you?" and to report on those who suffered loss of property or life as a consequence of their faith.

The initial documents that articulated a vision of the community that Friends sought to establish were the *Epistle of the Elders of Balby* (1656), as already mentioned, and *The Testimony of the Brethren* (1666) as Friends sought to adhere to what Fox in 1670 called "the ancient principles of truth." They sometimes talked about Gospel Order. This meant organizing everyday affairs in a way that reflected the original harmony between creator and creation. Friends used the phrase "to describe the nature of church and society as lived by a community reconciled and in right relationship with God and each other" (Lloyd Lee Wilson, in Abbott, et al., 2012, p. 15). In trying to live up to the ideal, Friends developed expectations of behavior, ways to sustain a unified public stance, and procedures to manage internal disputes. They also asserted the authority of the gathered body over the inspired individual, setting up procedures for dealing with "disorderly walkers" whose beliefs and behaviors were out of line with those of the community and threatened to bring down increased persecution. The Elders of Balby ended their letter with a statement drawn from Paul's letter to the Corinthians: "These things we do not lay upon you as a rule or form to walk by; but that all, with a measure of the light, which is pure and holy, may be guided: and so in the light walking and abiding, these things may be fulfilled in the Spirit, not in the letter, for the letter killeth, but the Spirit giveth life." This statement is included in the books of *Faith and Practice* of most liberal Quaker meetings and used to express their resistance to centralized authority.

The movement grew despite persecution and the legal prohibition of Quaker worship. A growing Quaker presence in London, and that city's centrality to British communication networks, made it first an alternative focus to Swarthmoor Hall and then the dominant center. Friends organized London Yearly Meeting as a formal coordinating body for local meetings around the country. It is now known as Britain Yearly Meeting and is a reference point for much of world Quakerism.

Meanwhile, Friends were traveling abroad and gaining adherents in the Netherlands and Germany. The intrepid Mary Fisher, a former servant and early convert, was one of the first Friends to cross the Atlantic to Barbados. She then went to Massachusetts, where she was promptly imprisoned and bundled back to England on the next ship. Undeterred, she decided in 1657 that she was going to meet the teenaged Sultan Mehmet IV of Turkey. She faced down reluctant sea captains and traveled hundreds of miles overland to Adrianople (north of Constantinople/Istanbul). Her audacity earned her an audience with Mehmet IV and his advisors; she said they listened more politely than many in England. She declined an offer to remain at his court but reported that "the seed of them is near unto God." The Sultan's decision two years later to allow the translation of the Bible into Turkish may have reflected those conversations.

The seventeenth century had no podcasts, op-eds, or opinionated television commentators to weigh in on public disputes. Instead, there were raucous face-to-face debates and pamphlet wars in which opponents assailed each other on the pages of badly printed tracts and books that sometimes went through multiple editions. As the Quaker movement grew, angry clergymen mounted attacks. The titles are often more engaging than the contents. The prominent Rhode Island Baptist Roger Williams condemned Quakers in *Fox Digged Out of His Burrouugh* [Burrow], prompting Fox himself to fight back with *A Lying New England Firebrand Quenched*. Long before he became famous for founding Pennsylvania, the young William Penn, who had become a convinced Quaker at age 22, was one of their leading "opinionists." Often writing in prison, he defended Friends against the charge that they were not Christians. His book *No Cross, No Crown* grew from a few dozen pages to hundreds over several editions.[2] Robert Barclay's formidable *Apology* (1676) systematically connected Quakerism to Christianity in scholarly Latin. The full title in its English version was: *An Apology for the true Christian Divinity, as the same is held forth and preached by the people called, in scorn, Quakers; being a full Explanation and Vindication of their Principles and Doctrines, by many Arguments deduced from Scripture and right reason, and the testimonies of famous Authors, both ancient and modern, with a full Answer to the strongest Objections usually made against them; presented to the King; written and published, in Latin, for the information of Strangers, by Robert Barclay; and now put into our own Language, for the benefit of his Countrymen.*

Quakers hurled pamphlets at each other as well as the authorities. The movement drew people who found the emphasis on direct revelation exhilarating but who wanted nobody else to tell them what to do or say or even when to meet for worship. They disliked what they called "Foxism": the efforts of Fox, Fell, and others to provide structure and coherence to the movement. Church governance created stability, but internal conflicts still arose, in part because Fox was not always charitable toward his opponents. George Keith was one example of an early leader who began challenging central teachings and urged adoption of a creed. After being disowned by Philadelphia Friends in 1692 for his combativeness and divisiveness, he later became a priest in the Church of England.

In the mid-1660s, Friends in different parts of England began regular correspondence, sharing both practical and spiritual advice. The "Morning Meeting" was a group of leading Friends who began to meet in 1673 in London on every second day (Monday) morning to supervise traveling ministers and approve publications. They were willing to impose censorship in the interest of a consistent message. Another important outcome was the "Meeting for Sufferings," a committee organized in 1668 to petition the government to alleviate the suffering of Friends who had been imprisoned or lost their property. It soon became a clearing house for information about Friends who were tangled in legal problems or mired in poverty. The name survives for the executive committee of Britain Yearly Meeting.

QUAKERS IN THE NEW WORLD

When William Penn stepped ashore in the new colony of Pennsylvania in October 1682, he became the most famous Quaker in the Americas then and arguably ever since. After all, no other bronze Quaker stands 37 feet tall atop a city hall at the center of a metropolis of millions. Penn's prominent role in the growing colonies in the 1680s stood in sharp contrast to the situation only 20 years earlier when Massachusetts authorities had executed the Boston martyrs—Marmaduke Stephenson and William Robinson in 1659, Mary Dyer in 1660, and William Leddra in 1661. It shows how quickly the Society of Friends was winning grudging acceptance after the initial hostility and persecution.

Penn himself was a bit of a late arrival in America, having sent deputies ahead the previous year to get the colony started. A Quaker presence had been growing in other English colonies for more than two decades. George Fox traveled and preached in the New World over three years in the early 1660s. There were Quakers in the Caribbean colonies of Jamaica and Barbados, in Virginia and the Carolinas, and on both sides of Long Island Sound in Rhode Island and New York. A handful of Friends in Flushing, New York, then governed by the Dutch, petitioned New Netherlands Governor Peter Stuyvesant in 1657 to request religious tolerance for themselves and others. Known as the Flushing Remonstrance this became the first American argument for freedom of religion. Quakers in Newport, Rhode Island laid the groundwork for New England Yearly Meeting in 1661.

Quakers were particularly prominent in what is now the state of New Jersey, and actually introduced Penn to the American scene. After Charles II granted West Jersey to a group of Quaker proprietors in 1675, Penn helped to sort out their competing claims and planned for Quaker settlement, including the town of Burlington on the east side bank of the Delaware River about 15 miles upstream from the future Philadelphia. In 1682, while actively engaged with Pennsylvania, he and 11 associates bought the proprietary rights to East Jersey and encouraged Quakers to settle there; Robert Barclay, the Quaker theologian, served as governor of East Jersey and arranged the settlement of the town of Perth Amboy as its first capital.

Proprietary colonies were essentially giant real estate deals. Under English law, proprietors were granted the *English* property rights to a chunk of the New World. They were expected to purchase land rights from the local native peoples, although the deals were one-sided and the requirement seldom enforced. They could then resell that land to other settlers at a markup—as long as the French in Canada or the Spanish in Florida or the Native peoples themselves didn't interfere with English control. That is the deal that William Penn got from Charles II in March 1681. In return for cancelling a very substantial debt that the crown owed to his father, a very successful and prominent admiral, Penn received the title to what were potentially tens of millions of acres of lands stretching westward from the west bank of the Delaware River. The king not only settled a debt but also filled a strategic gap in settlement between Maryland and New Jersey, expecting English settlers to push aside the scattering of Swedes, Finns, and Dutch who were already there, and who were themselves displacing Native Americans.

After naming his new landholding for his father, Penn decided that he wanted it to start with something more than a straggling settlement. He instructed his agents in the new colony on the particulars for Philadelphia. They were to pick a site that was high, dry, healthy, and had good moorage in the Delaware River, and were to make streets "uniform down to the river." Houses were to be sited in the middle of building lots to slow the spread of fires of the sorts that had repeatedly ravaged London and create a "green country town." Squares were set off in the city center and at the center of each quadrant—spaces that remain basic to Philadelphia's character today. The plan anticipated the American penchant for growth. Streets were unusually wide and Penn made sure that the expansive plan extended from the Delaware to the Schuylkill River "that we might have room for present and after Commers."

A Philadelphia built for growth fit two of Penn's purposes, for he was both an English expansionist and a businessman in severe need of cash. But there was a third and deeper reason as well. Historians often quote Penn's statement that Pennsylvania was a "Holy Experiment," although he used the term only once in a private letter. He never used the phrase in promoting the colony, which he presented as a land of economic opportunity and good investment prospects where all Christians would find opportunity to worship as they pleased. What he likely meant by "holy experiment" was an exercise or trial of broad religious toleration. Pennsylvania was not to be a comprehensive utopia, but a liberal or enlightened Christian society whose goal of religious freedom was a reaction to the religious intolerance of seventeenth-century Britain and Europe that so hindered the lives of Quakers.

Penn believed in democratic institutions, establishing and working with representative bodies, even when they had minds of their own. In the Charter of Privileges that he issued in 1701, he accepted limits on his personal authority. But he began the document with a provision that confirmed liberty of conscience to all who believed in God and pledged to "live quietly under civil government." Office holding was restricted to Christians. This provision of toleration was the only one that could not be amended or removed. Europe during Penn's lifetime was wracked by religious wars and the persecution of people who dissented from the state religion. England's restrictions on freedom of worship had been the central challenge for Quakers through the 1660s and 1670s. To Penn, the holy experiment was tolerance for all forms of Christian belief and worship, giving Quakers freedom of belief but not a privileged position.

Efforts at fair dealing extended to the initial Quaker interaction with the Native Americans of Pennsylvania. Penn sought to work honestly with the Lenape (or Delaware) people and to properly purchase lands before opening them to British settlers. The most famous episode, however, likely never happened. In 1771, Benjamin West painted William Penn in 1683 making a treaty with the Lenape under a spreading elm tree at Shackamaxon on the Delaware just north of Philadelphia. Quaker painter Edward Hicks revisited this image several times in the 1840s. Sad to say, there is no recorded evidence that the meeting under the Treaty Elm ever took place, although it was good propaganda in the hands of Hicks, who surely thought he was depicting a real event.

Compared to the more violent Puritans of New England, the first generation of American Friends look good, if not perfect. Even the good start would not last. In 1737 William Penn's son Thomas, by then Anglican rather than Quaker, worked with other

Pennsylvanians to defraud the Lenape. The notorious Walking Purchase manipulated what the Lenape thought was a straightforward agreement to sell rights to as much land as a man could walk around in a day. The younger Penn prepared a pathway through the forest, hired the three fastest runners in the colony, and then finagled the resulting boundaries even further, gaining a vastly larger chunk of northeastern Pennsylvania than the Lenape intended. Even with this fraud, relations between the new settlers and the original residents remained relatively peaceful until the war with France and its Native allies in the 1750s.

William Penn was long gone from America before relations with the Lenape turned sour. He spent only two years in Pennsylvania before a land dispute took him back to London in 1683. Penn and Charles Calvert, the proprietor of Maryland, both claimed the "lower counties" along the Delaware River, now the state of Delaware, lands that were highly desirable because of their convenience to the river. Penn won the decision but decided to stay in England because his friendship with the new king James II gave him an opening to advance religious toleration. The Glorious Revolution that replaced James with William III and Mary II knocked Penn's fortunes for a loop. He was not able to return to Pennsylvania until 1699. He departed again within two years, leaving his colony and its Quakers to grow and prosper on their own. Penn died in England in 1718. Philadelphia grew into the most important city in the British colonies. The vexing dispute with Maryland persisted until Charles Mason and Jeremiah Dixon surveyed Pennsylvania's southern boundary in the 1760s.

William Penn was a man of contradictions, both insider and outsider. He was a son of privilege who defied his father to join a movement of ordinary people. He advocated liberty of conscience but owned slaves, as did many other early Quakers in Pennsylvania. He is a towering figure in American history (and literally towering in Philadelphia) who spent only four years on American soil. He understood the virtues of simplicity but could not resist the impulse to live like a grandee and spent time imprisoned for debt. He used his access to the highest people in England to advance the interests of a scorned minority. He was, in other words, a powerful, passionate, and flawed individual.

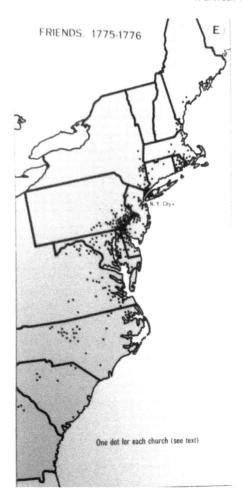

FRIENDS, 1775-1776

One dot for each church (see text)

Figure 2.2 Quaker meetings in British North America in 1775–76. At the time of the American Revolution, Quakers concentrated in the middle colonies of New Jersey, Pennsylvania, Delaware, and Maryland, with smaller clusters in Rhode Island and North Carolina and on Long Island (New York)

Source: C.O. Paullin, *Atlas of the Historical Geography of the United States* (Washington: Carnegie Institution, 1932)

THEOLOGICAL RADICALS

Friends experienced the Power of the Lord as governing their lives and relationships with all people. Their way of worship, sitting in expectant silence awaiting divine guidance, set them apart from the state-controlled church of seventeenth-century England to the degree that Parliament viewed them as a threat to the well-being of the state. They were theological radicals who centered their beliefs on a theology that was both prophetic and mystical. They highlighted the direct accessibility and guidance of God and a style of worship that facilitated direct communion with the Light of Christ. They were not modern radicals agitating for social and economic change as primary goals (and not like their contemporaries the Diggers who advocated a sort of communism). At the same time, they saw and acted on the socially radical implications of that theology.

Within a century of their founding, Quakers had shifted from being a heavily persecuted radical movement determined to re-establish "primitive" or original Christianity to a well-established, yet distinctive body whose members were central to governance and commerce in the American colonies. In England, the stringent laws that led to the persecution of Friends gradually eased by the start of the eighteenth century but Friends sought to remain a people apart and resisted being drawn into the wider culture and its pressures to amass wealth and status. Between 1666 and 1668, much was done to organize local and regional meetings, manage the internal affairs of the community, and present a unified face to the world. As Friends entered what became known as the "quietist period" in the eighteenth century, outsiders remained leery of their unorthodox theology that stressed obedience to Christ and subjugation of the "creaturely activity" (or human will). Those beliefs would set Friends apart from society even as they set the groundwork for social reform, radical action to end slavery, and reluctance to participate in the violence of the American Revolution.

NOTES

1 It was not only early Quakers who suffered from hostile governments. The first Uganda Friends Church was founded in Kampala in 1948. However, the dictator Idi Amin banned Friends from the country in 1973, destroying

many of their churches and forcing members to flee the nation. A remnant of the Friends Church continued to meet in secret. Gradual restoration of peace only came after the end of Idi Amin's rule in 1980.

2 Penn also played an important role in the development of legal rights. In 1670 he was arrested for violating the Conventicle Act, which prohibited religious gatherings of more than five unrelated people outside the rules of the Church of England, effectively outlawing Quaker meetings. The jurors for his trial, with co-defendant William Mead, courageously established the principle that a jury makes an independent decision and cannot be forced by a judge to return a specific verdict.

FURTHER READING

Michael L. Birkel, *Engaging Scripture: Reading the Bible with Early Friends* (Richmond, IN: Friends United Press, 2005). The author delves into the ways in which biblical knowledge and references were essential to early Friends.

Rosemary Moore, *The Light in Their Consciences: The Early Quakers in Britain 1646–1666* (University Park, PA: The Pennsylvania State University Press, 2000). The best detailed introduction to the lives and beliefs of the earliest Friends.

Andrew Murphy, *William Penn: A Life* (New York: Oxford University Press, 2018). A comprehensive biography that shows Penn's complexities and contradictions.

John Punshon, *A Portrait in Grey* (London: Quaker Books, 2006). A readable introduction to the origins and growth of Quakerism by a leading British Friend.

A PECULIAR AND
CONTRADICTORY PEOPLE
THE EIGHTEENTH AND NINETEENTH
CENTURIES

Early Quakers declared that they were "a peculiar people." In the twenty-first century to call someone "peculiar" suggests that they are odd, unusual, or downright strange. When Quakers embraced the term, however, they meant something very different. Their reference was the New Testament passage in I Peter 2:9, which reads, in the King James translation:

> But ye are a chosen generation, a royal priesthood, an holy nation, a peculiar people; that ye should shew forth the praises of him who hath called you out of darkness into his marvelous light;

In the New Revised Standard Version the main difference in translation is to refer to "God's own people" rather than "a peculiar people." Similarly, the epistle of Titus says that Jesus Christ "gave himself to us, that he might redeem himself from all iniquity, and purify unto himself a peculiar people, zealous of good works" (Titus 2:14). As this "peculiar people," in other words, Quakers were a special group who were trying to live sober, righteous, and godly lives. Modern translations of the same Bible passage talk about a special people, or a pure people, or "a people of his own who are zealous for good deeds"—all translations that help modern readers understand what the early Friends meant.

The term has stuck nevertheless, used by Quakers and non-Quakers alike. It also morphed into "peculiarities," referring to the distinctive behaviors that set early Quakers apart in their plain clothing, plain speaking, scorn of worldly amusements, and refusal of oath taking. These increasingly eccentric behaviors (also known as Quaker "distinctives") were a way for Quakers to express their idea of true Christian conduct and to maintain their purity. They also isolated Friends from their larger society. Expansion in Britain and parts of northeastern America slowed substantially in the eighteenth century. Quakers as an organized group withdrew from Pennsylvania politics in the face of heavy pressure to levy taxes for warfare. Increasingly inward-focused Quakers in the United States fought fierce theological battles in the early nineteenth century that created organizational splits and divisions.

To focus only on declining attendance and the increasing preponderance of gray heads in older British or American meetings, whether in the eighteenth or twenty-first centuries, however, is to miss much of the story. Quakers and Quakerism did not move on a single track. Nineteenth-century Quakerism remained a vital religion that expanded and evolved as it spread westward with English-speaking settlers in the United States and as Quakers from both sides of the Atlantic began missionary work in Africa and Asia. Individual Quakers were innovators in the development of British and American industry, business, and science. Once their meetings were free of slave-holders they also built on the anti-slavery work of John Woolman in the 1700s to play leading roles in a wide range of progressive causes such as the abolition of slavery and prison reform. Quaker men were increasingly seen as hidebound and conservative, yet nineteenth-century Quaker women stepped forth to lead the women's rights movement and other reforms.

This chapter begins with two sections that outline the internal development of the Society of Friends as a religion spanning the North Atlantic Ocean. We look at the development of formal organization and the challenge of slavery in the eighteenth century and painful divisions among American Quakers in the nineteenth century. The third section maintains the internal focus, describing the spread of Quakerism into the American West and the beginnings of missionary work. The last two sections supplement this chronological story by exploring two ways in which Friends interacted and influenced the wider world through their achievements in science and business and their work as progressive reformers. A final section contrasts divergent paths that emerged in the late nineteenth century and sets the stage for Chapter 4 about the development of Quakerism as a worldwide religion in the twentieth century.

Having already explored the distinct meaning of "peculiar people," we also want to briefly unpack the implications of "contradictory people" that run through the chapter. One of the contradictions is the fact that Quakers grew increasingly influential

Table 3.1 Key dates for Quakerism in the eighteenth and nineteenth centuries

1691/94	Death of George Fox; Publication of George Fox's Journal.
1702	Death of Margaret Fell.
1756	Quakers relinquish control of Pennsylvania legislature.
1758	Philadelphia Yearly Meeting condemns slaveholding by Friends.
1816	First Peace Society in Britain founded by William Allen and Joseph T. Price.
1827–28	The "Great Separation" in North America into Hicksite and Orthodox branches.
1843	John Bright enters British Parliament.
1845	Gurneyite–Wilburite separation in New England.
1846	Levi Coffin settles in Cincinnati, Ohio, and becomes known as "president" of the Underground Railroad.
1848	Lucretia Mott initiates organization of the first women's rights convention in Seneca Falls, New York.
1869	American Friends undertake supervision of Indian Agencies in Nebraska, Kansas, and Indian Territories; New England Yearly Meeting sends missionaries to Ramallah, Palestine, and establishes a school for girls.
1871	Friends Foreign Mission Association established in Britain; Indiana Yearly Meeting Foreign Missionary Association established.
1886	Iowa Yearly Meeting is first to formally accept pastoral system.
1887	Richmond Declaration of Faith adopted by most Gurneyite North American yearly meetings.
1895	Manchester Conference held in England.
1900	Friends General Conference (FGC) established.
1902	Five Years Meeting (renamed Friends United Meeting or FUM in 1965) established.

in society at large even as their numbers stabilized and they lost their dynamism as a revolutionary religion. Starting from a strong sense of unity built on a London–Philadelphia axis American Friends splintered on the basis of belief, despite the initial scorn of the founding generations for strict theology. A third contrast is differing responses to rigid and uncharitable Christianity. Early Friends, sought to recover the pure Christianity of the first and second centuries, whereas some modern liberal Friends reject Christianity altogether.

ATLANTIC QUAKERISM IN THE EIGHTEENTH CENTURY

The Society of Friends in the eighteenth century was bound together by common belief and by the Atlantic Ocean. Thousands of Quakers made a single voyage from England to the colonies as permanent settlers, but many others crossed back and forth as merchants and as traveling ministers. William Penn, for one prominent example, made the tedious six-week voyage from England to Pennsylvania in 1682 and then back in 1684 to defend his claim against challenges, returned to his estate on the Delaware River in 1699, and then reversed again in 1701 to spend his final years in Britain. Seeking to ensure that scattered Friends did not stray from central Quaker tenets, London Yearly Meeting sent carefully selected books and pamphlets to America and the Caribbean (especially those by Robert Barclay and William Penn). They also gave official blessing to Friends who made the westward voyage across the Atlantic. American Quakers such as John Woolman in turn shared their ministry in England.

At the same time that Quakers on both sides of the Atlantic tried to maintain connections with each other, they also tended to erect a "hedge" between themselves and the broader society in which they were situated. With the fervor of the first generations fading away, and the erosion of political power in Pennsylvania, Friends turned their attention to enforcing consistent practices and avoiding the temptations of the surrounding culture. The era is sometimes called the "Quietist period," referring both to a slow disengagement from the world of politics and to spiritual practice that emphasized a contemplative spiritual life and drew on the writings of contemporary Christian mystics. Quietist Friends who waited diligently for inward clarity would have seemed remarkably passive to George Fox or the Valiant Sixty. Distrust of one's own impulses could lead to extremes—one Quaker took 23 years of prayerful consideration before being certain that her intended husband was the right choice and not just a passing fancy!

Friends systematized and enforced membership. Early Friends knew who they were through close interaction and the channels of communication that they developed to resist persecution. By the 1700s, however, Quakers in the colonies wanted London Yearly Meeting to certify that emigrants were in good standing with their home meeting, not to mention that they were trustworthy in business and weren't leaving a wife and family behind. British Quakers began to create membership lists in the 1730s to distinguish between genuine adherents to the Society of Friends, who merited financial help in times of need, and unscrupulous individuals who claimed to be Quakers purely to benefit from charity. Early Friends had come to Quakerism through direct spiritual experience and convincement. Now the solidification of an individualistic movement into a settled religious community raised the question of the status of children who might grow to adulthood conforming to Quaker practice without an intense personal transformation. The solution was to create a category of "birthright membership" that allowed children of Quaker families to be considered full members.

Quakers tried to maintain their distance from worldly temptations as they waited for God's rule to come on earth. They avoided distractions and vanities—no music, dancing, card-playing, or reading frivolous books. Plain speech, which carried a strong message of social equality in the 1660s, became increasingly quaint as the decades passed and "thee" and "thou" faded from use by the general public. Especially in North America, plain clothing became a standardized "uniform." Men wore grey or dark brown suits topped with black broad-brimmed hats. Women wore drably colored dresses and bonnets.

Meetings enforced superficial "distinctives" through social pressure, but they disowned members for a wide range of behaviors that either disrupted the Society of Friends or brought it into disrepute. As Quaker scholar Pink Dandelion has summarized, disownment was intended to protect spiritual purity by fending off contaminating influences while also signaling that purity to the outside world. Historian Jack Marietta cataloged 44 different types of offenses for which Philadelphia area Friends could be held accountable and often disowned in the years from 1682 to 1776. Drunkenness, sexual promiscuity, and fraud in business were obvious problems visible to the larger public. Internal problems revolved around the personal conflicts that inevitably arose in small, tightknit groups. Friends who quarreled and rejected the arbitration of their Meeting were likely to find themselves on the outside. Most troublesome was the question of marriage. Friends were expected to marry other Friends, and only with the approval ("under the care") of their parents and Meetings. The Philadelphia data show 4,925 cases in which individuals were charged with marrying outside of the Quaker community over that 94-year time span—about 50 per year—with almost half leading to disownment.

BOX 3.1   QUAKER DISTINCTIVES

Members of the Society of Friends in the 1700s and 1800s developed a number of distinctive practices that expressed their testimony to God's truth and that set them apart as a special people. The common characteristic was an emphasis on simplicity and plainness as a way to protest and avoid the empty customs and temptations of the world.

Plain speech: Friends refused to use titles when addressing a superior, using plain Charles Stuart for King Charles II and arguing that terms like "Your Grace" and "Lord" should be reserved for Jesus Christ. Speakers of seventeenth-century English used "you" when addressing equals and superiors and "thee/thou" when speaking to a subordinate. Friends instead used "thee" and "thou" in all circumstances to recognize the equality of all people, emphasizing humility before God. They also thought that the use of "you" as both plural and singular was confusing and thus violated the testimony of integrity, hence another reason to prefer singular "thee/thou."

Plain dress: Early Friends dressed in plain clothing to demonstrate their disdain for vain displays of wealth and status. Clothing choices that were plain but common in the early years evolved into a standard that was increasingly old-fashioned and eccentric.

Times and seasons: Early Friends refused to use the "world's names" for days or the week and months of the year because many derived from pagan gods or even honored individuals (like July for Julius Caesar). Sunday became "first day," January became "first month," and so on through the calendar.

Festivals and celebrations: Because all days are holy, early Friends did not celebrate religious holidays, nor did they celebrate individual birthdays.

Practices that sent an easily recognized social message in the early decades rigidified and looked increasingly quaint and eccentric by the later 1800s, gradually dropping out of use. Marge's grandmother, for example, used "thee/thou" among other Quakers of her generation but easily switched to standard twentieth-century language in other circumstances. A holdover is that many meetings still offer "First Day School" rather than "Sunday School" for their children.

The inward turn extended to politics. Quakers played a major role in Pennsylvania's colonial politics in its early decades, although they were caught in a power struggle among William Penn's descendants, Quaker merchants, and non-Quaker settlers. Individual Quakers also served as governors of Rhode Island, New Jersey, and North Carolina. The early Pennsylvania Assembly refused to create a militia, and it voted for war taxes only with the stipulation that the funds be used to feed local Native Americans.

British General William Braddock's stunning 1755 defeat in western Pennsylvania at the start of the Seven Years War (or French and Indian War in the United States) triggered a crisis. Philadelphia Yearly Meeting pressured members to resign from the Assembly after it voted for a war tax and established a militia, leaving politically active Quakers a minority in the "Quaker colony." Twenty years later, when the colonies chose open rebellion against British authority and declared independence, the Society adopted strict neutrality. They refused to affirm loyalty to either side at considerable personal and economic cost. Roughly one-fifth of eligible Quaker men did take up arms and were disowned, and the Society of Friends was effectively sidelined from the politics of nation building after the Revolution.

The Quaker response to slavery—perhaps the most enduring legacy of the Quietist years—demonstrates the strengths as well as weakness of the Quaker approach to social change. In the eighteenth and early nineteenth centuries they were leaders in efforts to abolish slavery. When viewed with twenty-first-century eyes, they are also disappointing, for that leadership seems a slow and halting process. Friends who took up this vitally important concern focused for many years on aligning their own practices with their beliefs before turning to broader work to abolish slavery completely. In both the rural South and urban North, Quakers arrived in colonies where slavery was part of the established economic system, and some of them acquired slaves. Slavery was fundamental the Caribbean sugar colonies of Jamaica and Barbados where Friends made thousands of converts in the 1650s and 1660s, and there were Quaker merchants in Rhode Island, New York, and Pennsylvania who were involved in the slave trade.

One of the paradoxes of the Quakers and slavery is found in the history of Barbados, a Caribbean island sometimes called the "Nursery of Truth" because of its large number of Friends in the later seventeenth century. George Fox, visiting in 1670, had encouraged Friends to see slaves as spiritual equals and to worship with them in their households. He had also drawn on his understanding of slavery as it existed in the Roman world to suggest in a sermon on family order that slaves be freed after a period of service. Not surprisingly, English families and slaves worshipping together alarmed the authorities who forbade such mixed gatherings. As historian Katherine Gerbner notes, however, these Quakers acted on a belief in the *spiritual* equality of all Christians rather than on modern convictions of full equality. Nevertheless, Quakers and other missionizing groups undermined the English assumption that it was permissible to enslave heathens but not Christians. If slaves professed Quakerism or other forms of Christianity, then another justification for slavery had to be found—the new distinction between "white" and "Black."

Irish Friend and prominent traveling minister, William Edmundson, condemned slavery as early as 1675, and in 1688, a group of German and Dutch Quakers living in a village outside Philadelphia broadcast what is known as the Germantown Protest, the first public condemnation of slavery by white North Americans. Friends are justly proud of the Germantown Protest, which drew on the uneasiness with slavery of early Quakers like George Fox. However, the cause was too controversial for other meetings to take up and it went nowhere—except the archives of the Haverford College Library.

Friends also caused discomfort by asserting the spiritual equality of Native peoples. In Fox's 1672 trip to the colonies, he reports several meetings with the Native leaders, and an encounter at an official's house with a doctor who argued that the local people knew nothing of the Light. Fox demonstrated that this was not true and made the doctor ashamed in the eyes of the governor.

A generation later, Quaker Benjamin Lay was fierce and dramatic, pulling no punches in writing *All Slave-keepers that keep the Innocent in Bondage, Apostates*. He refused to use any product made by slave labor and liked striking gestures. He once showed up at Philadelphia Yearly Meeting dressed as a soldier, delivered an anti-slavery sermon buttressed with Bible verses, and then plunged a sword into the Bible and skewered a bladder filled with blood. The sober-sided Quakers in attendance were not amused and several meetings disowned him.

Where Benjamin Lay was fierce, John Woolman was gentle but unrelenting in laboring with Friends and others over the immorality of slaveholding. Committed as well to the rights of Native Americans and to a life of simplicity, he began his anti-slavery ministry by refusing to assist in writing a will that included slaves as heritable property. Over several decades, he traveled in the ministry, visiting meetings and individuals and quietly but insistently arguing the basic immorality of human bondage. He was reserved in manner but tireless in pressing his radical arguments about the corrupting effects of slavery on everyone involved. When visiting a slave owner, he paid the slaves who served him out of his own pocket. He also had a deep concern about economic inequality. His essay "A Plea for the Poor" was a pioneering effort to understand the roots of poverty. He refused to wear dyed clothing after he learned that dye workers were often harmed by noxious chemicals. Late in life he gave up riding in stagecoaches because of the cruel treatment of the horses. *The Journal of John Woolman*, a record of his spiritual life, has been a classic of American literature since its first publication in 1774.

The basic change in Quaker practice came after 1750. In 1753, Philadelphia Yearly Meeting republished Woolman's anti-slavery pamphlet *Some Considerations on the Keeping of Negroes*, giving a seal of approval to its sentiments. Over the next three decades, the six yearly meetings in North America, from the Carolinas to New England, repudiated slavery. In some cases they started with prohibitions on Friends engaging in buying and selling of slaves, before adding the requirement that anyone who owned slaves must make arrangements to free them or lose their membership. Some meetings in the Southern colonies took the further step of buying freedom for slaves of nonmembers. This focus on practices within the Quaker community may actually have helped them move the issue forward within the larger society, since they could make themselves examples of positive change without becoming entangled in broad political debates.

The praise Quakers receive for acting in advance of other Americans must be tempered by the reality that they remained children of their times. Even after making slave ownership a cause for disownment they remained unwilling to accept African Americans as members until the 1780s. Most were even slower to accept people of African heritage as social equals or guests in their homes. Not until the era of the American Revolution and afterwards did Quakers move out of their quietist isolation and turn their efforts toward the comprehensive abolition of slavery in the larger society. A key figure is Anthony Benezet, who started a school for free Blacks in 1770, founded the first American anti-slavery organization in 1775, and helped to persuade Pennsylvania to adopt phased emancipation in 1780. All the other Northern states had followed by 1804. In 1790, Philadelphia Yearly Meeting petitioned Congress to abolish slavery nationwide. These actions in the last quarter of the century mark a transition from an era in which Quakers emphasized living up to their own standards to one in which many Friends were increasingly active in trying to change the world.

British Quakers followed a similar path. Quiet anti-slavery efforts among Friends themselves went public after the American colonies gained independence and the Northern states debated and began to eliminate slavery. London Yearly Meeting had prohibited members from engaging in the slave trade in the 1760s, but the goal was to maintain the purity of the group. In 1783, however,

David Barclay led a delegation of Quakers to urge the Board of Trade to consider anti-slavery petitions (there seems to have been a growing sense of competition between American and British Friends to demonstrate their moral standing). Four years later nine of the twelve men who met in a London printing shop to found Britain's Abolition Society were Quakers, starting a movement that quickly grew beyond the Society of Friends but retained close ties with it.

BOX 3.2   JOHN WOOLMAN'S TESTIMONY AGAINST SLAVERY

John Woolman (1720–72) was a New Jersey Quaker who wrote and spoke publicly against slavery as destructive to everyone involved. He also took opportunities to reason directly with individual slave owners, whether staying in a slave-owning house on his travels or refusing to help someone pass slaves to their heirs.

About this time an ancient man of good esteem in the neighbourhood came to my house to get his will written. He had young negroes, and I asked him privately how he purposed to dispose of them. He told me. I then said, 'I cannot write thy will without breaking my own peace,' and respectfully gave him my reasons for it. He signified that he had a choice that I should have written it, but as I could not, consistently with my conscience, he did not desire it, and so he got it written by some other person. A few years after, there being great alterations in his family, he came again to get me to write his will. His negroes were yet young, and his son, to whom he intended to give them, was, since he first spoke to me, from a libertine become a sober young man, and he supposed that I would have been free on that account to write it. We had much friendly talk on the subject, and then deferred it. A few days after he came again and directed their freedom, and I then wrote his will.

Near the time that the last-mentioned Friend first spoke to me, a neighbour received a bad bruise in his body and sent for me to bleed him, which having done, he desired me to write his will. I took notes, and amongst other things he told me to

> which of his children he gave his young negro. I considered the pain and distress he was in, and knew not how it would end, so I wrote his will, save only that part concerning his slave, and carrying it to his bedside, read it to him. I then told him in a friendly way that I could not write any instruments by which my fellow-creatures were made slaves, without bringing trouble on my own mind. I let him know that I charged nothing for what I had done, and desired to be excused from doing the other part in the way he proposed. We then had a serious conference on the subject; at length, he agreeing to set her free, I finished his will.

ATLANTIC QUAKERS IN THE NINETEENTH CENTURY

The late Quietist period was a time when some meetings lost members and felt a lack of vibrant ministry. In addition, the strict discipline drove many young people out of the Society. The evangelical renewal of the Second Great Awakening (ca. 1795–1830) affected Friends by stirring up new interest in biblical literacy and conformity of belief even as disagreements became more pronounced. In the Americas, views on Christ and the Bible led to controversies and divisions. In the United Kingdom, most Friends embraced an evangelical theology, and no major schisms occurred. The Society there opened to the wider world while retaining the style of worship in which ministry arose out of the silence. The start of the century was filled with the energy of successful industrialists. Other Friends were pioneers for social justice. Elizabeth Fry, whose face appeared on the British five-pound note from 2002 to 2017, was a major figure in initiating prison reform in Britain, and American Warner Mifflin originated the idea of paying reparations to freed slaves.

The complex pressures of the new nation, however, stretched Friends' meetings in North America to the breaking point. In 1827 disagreements over theology and church governance combined with strong personalities and rural/urban divisions to create a potent mix that blew up into the Great Separation between Orthodox and Hicksite Quakers. Elias Hicks, whose name became associated with one group, was a charismatic minister from New York. A farmer and surveyor and an ardent opponent of slavery,

Hicks preached that the Inward Light of Christ was more central to faith than the authority of Scripture and rejected the orthodox Christian doctrine of atonement. While Hicks was the most prominent dissenter, the Hicksites were in fact united largely in their opposition to the Orthodox, not in matters of theology.

The Orthodox body drew Friends who had formed close ties with non-Quaker evangelicals in philanthropic and reform work. These Friends valued a more orthodox Christian theology, strongly asserting the authority of the Bible over that of the Inward Light and emphasizing the divinity of Christ. They distrusted the Hicksites as coming too close to Unitarianism. English Friend John Joseph Gurney, a prominent businessman, social reformer, and erudite Bible scholar, was an important influence. He argued vigorously and articulately for a Quakerism that was more evangelical in approach and more directly Bible-oriented—an emphasis that seemed to some Friends to be inconsistent with belief in the direct experience of the Holy Spirit. His approach pulled Friends in England and Ireland and many in the United States back toward regular Protestant Christianity. Nineteenth-century Quakers in England and Philadelphia supported organizations that published and distributed Bibles.

The split was social and economic as well as theological. The leaders among Orthodox Friends were city people, merchants and professionals who valued religious practices that were compatible with those of the middle-class Protestants with whom they associated. Hicksites tended to be country folk, sometimes with less formal education and less polished manners. Hicks himself used rural imagery to make his points. The theological difference and

Table 3.2 Contrasting Quakerisms

HICKSITE BELIEFS	GURNEY'S BELIEFS
Devotion to the Inward Light	Primacy of Bible over Inward Light
Toleration of dissent/freedom of thought	Justification and Sanctification as two events
Rejection of many Christian doctrines	Open to working with other Evangelicals
Continuing revelation	Emphasis on theological education

Source: based on Hamm (2003, p. 47)

the Hicksite challenge to the authority of Orthodox elders were central, but mutual distaste between different social classes and personalities played a role.

The upshot was two different groups claiming to be *the* Philadelphia Yearly Meeting. Hicksites had the numbers and the Orthodox had the money. Vehement debates sometimes split families. Control of meeting houses and property was contentious. Groups locked each other out. In some places the result was two meeting houses facing each other across a small plot of ground or a graveyard. The groups created separate colleges nine miles apart on the western outskirts of Philadelphia—Haverford College for the Orthodox and Swarthmore College for Hicksites. Similar separations occurred among Friends in Baltimore, Indiana, New York, and Ohio yearly meetings (where the debate culminated in very unQuakerly pushing and shoving). In contrast, Hopewell Meeting in Virginia split but the factions managed to share the same meetinghouse by worshiping at opposite ends of the building. The need for repairs finally forced them to squeeze back together, which turned out to be not so bad after all. Marge's grandmother, who was part of the Westbury, New York meeting, reminisced about carriages arriving on Sunday morning, stopping to drop people off at the Orthodox meeting house, and proceeding a few hundred feet further to drop other passengers at the adjacent Hicksite meetinghouse on the same property. Among Long Island Quakers, her Orthodox grandfather and Hicksite grandmother celebrated one of the first "mixed" marriages in 1913.

The separations among Friends in the eastern United States mended in bits in the decades after World War II whereas the more evangelical Friends pulled away from Midwestern meetings that increasingly accommodated modernism, eventually forming Evangelical Friends Alliance in 1965. Theologically conservative Friends founded what became Malone University and Barclay College, which have been important in training missionaries.[1]

The tendency for disagreements and separations continued among mid-century Quakers (see Figure 3.1). Progressive Friends (also known as Congregational Friends) split off from Hicksites. They included many abolitionists, women's rights advocates, temperance supporters, and peace activists, and freely engaged with non-Quakers who shared their concerns. Progressive Friends

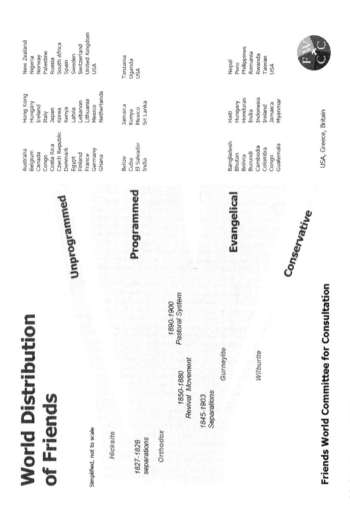

Figure 3.1 World distribution of Friends
Source: Courtesy of Friends World Committee for Consultation

rejected any hint of authority and hierarchy by abolishing elders, the recording of ministers, and separate men's and women's meetings. Although the group died out, their liberal approach influenced Hicksite meetings that eventually formed the core of Friends General Conference. Historian Thomas Hamm (2003, p. 46) argues that by the end of the nineteenth century "Hicksite Friends had achieved a new consensus about their faith … they openly described themselves as liberals, in sympathy with Unitarian and liberal movements in other Protestant denominations."

Meanwhile, the Orthodox branch suffered its own divisions. The catalyst was John Wilbur, from rural Rhode Island. He traveled tirelessly among Friends in the United States and Britain in the 1820s and 1830s, warning that the evangelical trend involved worldly compromises and undermined true Quakerism with its emphasis on direct access to the divine spirit. In effect, he wanted to return to his ideal of original Quakerism. In 1840, Wilbur traversed New England in the wake of one of Gurney's visits in an effort to counter that influence. The debate became increasingly heated and Wilbur led followers into their own yearly meeting in 1845. Further splits occurred in Baltimore and Ohio. A small number of Conservative Friends in the United States continue to maintain or "conserve" an early form of Quakerism that combines a strong Christian orientation with very simple practices.

These divisions and consolidations led to the formation of the three umbrella groupings to which most American Friends belong.

- *Friends General Conference*, a consultative and educational body, came together in 1900 to consolidate cooperative activities among Hicksite yearly meetings. Based in Philadelphia, it has expanded with the healing of the Hicksite–Orthodox split and the spread of unprogrammed meetings (see Glossary) around the country since the 1950s. Canadian Yearly Meeting is also affiliated and most Western European Friends would feel at home.
- *Friends United Meeting*, heavily concerned with missionary work, is based on Richmond, Indiana. It grew out of the Five Years Meeting, formed in 1902 to bring Orthodox and Gurneyite Friends under a common book of discipline that combined standard Christian theology with distinctive Quaker testimonies.

- *Evangelical Friends Church International* came together in the United States beginning in the 1940s and took on an international dimension in 1994. It is the most conservative on social issues and explicitly Christian like many FUM churches in its emphasis on the theology of the Richmond Declaration (see "Divergent paths" below) and George Fox's definition of Quaker Christianity in a 1671 letter to the Governor of Barbados. It places higher emphasis on the atonement and at times encouraging the outward sacraments and practices such as voting.

QUAKER EXPANSION

The interplay among Quakers in Britain and the eastern states that triggered the theological disputes and divisions was in some ways a sideshow. It occurred when the center of gravity of American Quakerism was shifting away from the Atlantic Coast and the Society of Friends was entering a new and very different era of growth. The white settlement of the American interior following the American Revolution took Friends into the Ohio Valley and points west. Quaker migrants were especially attracted by the Northwest Ordinance of 1787, which prohibited slavery north of the Ohio River. The largest numbers of Friends settled in Ohio and Indiana, some of whom left Virginia and the Carolinas to escape the surroundings of slavery. In turn, Friends from the Ohio Valley moved further west, particularly to Iowa and Oregon. Herbert Hoover, the first Quaker president, traced the trajectory—born in West Branch, Iowa in 1874 and moving to Newberg, Oregon in 1885. As historian Thomas Hamm points out, a majority of Orthodox Friends lived west of the Appalachian Mountains by 1843. They moved there for inexpensive land and for the potential to create holy communities apart from the worldly culture.

Religious revival fervor was part of the frontier experience, and Friends felt pressure to conform to the broader evangelical theology and practice. The rapid growth of Quakerism in the new communities meant that experienced Friends were spread thin. In response, Friends began to pay individuals to spend full time on care for new meetings. From this initial step toward a pastoral system, many Quaker meetings increasingly accepted new forms of worship that resembled their Protestant neighbors. The music and vocal prayers of revivals that appealed to younger Friends led to hymn-singing and Bible readings in addition to sermons by a designated pastor. Some Friends decided that it was acceptable to say Sunday School in place of First-Day School. By the last decades of the nineteenth century, roughly two-thirds of North American meetings hired pastors and listened to prepared messages. Some were beginning to identify as a Friends Church rather than a Friends Meeting.

Changes in belief accompanied changes in practice. After the American Civil War many Orthodox Friends experienced rapid and radical change. Those in the Philadelphia area increasingly focused on their own concerns, while those in other parts of the country came increasingly under the influence of the Wesleyan holiness movement. Beginning in the 1830s and peaking in the 1870s, the Holiness revival swept through many North American denominations. The possibility of "Christian Perfection" as enunciated by John Wesley, the founder of Methodism, was preached widely among the Methodists. The doctrine reached into Mennonite and Brethren communities and Quaker meetings in the Midwestern states and from there into Africa and South America. The potential for living the sinless sanctified life echoed the early Quaker doctrine of perfection, but in a new form that changed their meetings. The Holiness revivals excited young Quakers who were bored with their elders' reliance on silent waiting. The emphasis on "baptism of the Spirit" evoked a well-known experience among Friends. So did the blend of mysticism, social justice work, and recognition of women's right to preach.

The Holiness movement is still part of the evangelical Friends' consciousness. Philadelphia Quaker Hannah Whitall Smith became a central figure in both North American and British holiness circles and her book *The Christian's Secret of a Happy Life* remains in print as evangelical devotional reading. The Holiness tradition was strong in Oregon where the Quakers jointly formed Western Evangelical Seminary with the Church of the Nazarene, Church of God (Anderson), Free Methodists, and Wesleyans (it is now known as Portland Seminary at George Fox University). The Salvation Army was another closely connected body. In 1902 its international headquarters in London published *George Fox, The Red-Hot Quaker* by Staff-Captain Douglas, a book reprinted as recently as 2011.

Nineteenth-century Quakers also revived the practice of missionary outreach. Early Friends had tirelessly spread their message—the Valiant Sixty in England, George Fox in the Caribbean and North America, and many others crisscrossing continental Europe—but the impulse had weakened during the Quietist period. Mounting evangelicalism among Friends, however, stoked outreach and missionary efforts.

The British, who were more uniformly evangelical at this time, were among the first to establish missions. They began in their own communities with the establishment of Sunday evening programs that were part of a wider Adult Sunday School and home-mission movement. The programs combined instruction in reading and writing with hymn singing and Bible readings. They reached significant numbers of workers, tradesmen, and factory workers, but little effort was made to include them in regular Sunday morning worship or encourage them to seek membership. As many people may have been involved in the Adult Schools as in Quaker meetings by 1875.

From 1832 to 1838, James Backhouse and George Washington Walker travelled in Australia, establishing Quaker meetings that later formed the basis for Australia Yearly Meeting. Backhouse came from a wealthy English banking, railroad, and manufacturing family. He and Walker had the spiritual and financial support of their meetings. He was also concerned about the future of Australia's aboriginal peoples and the welfare of the many convicts who had been transported from England to Australia, working to reform the penal system there. Later in Cape Town, South Africa, he learned the Dutch language used by its settlers and established a multi-racial school for the poor.

Between 1850 and 1900 North American Gurneyite meetings began to send missionaries to many parts of the world, eventually establishing schools, hospitals and mission stations in Southern and Eastern Asia, East Africa, the Middle East, the Caribbean, and Alaska. Initially begun by Midwestern meetings energized by the revivals that moved younger Friends, the primary concern of this work was to bring people to Christ. Missionaries also valued literacy and actively supported translation of the Bible. Many of the missionaries were women, thus bringing with them and modeling the practice of women in ministry. The twentieth century brought a fresh round of mission work in East Africa, the African Great Lakes region, Central America, and South America, largely from yearly meetings influenced by these revivals (see Chapter 4).

BOX 3.3   QUAKER JOKES

The Quaker reputation for righteousness could attract skepticism. States like North Carolina and Indiana, where many Quakers lived in the nineteenth century, produced "Quaker jokes" that poked fun at their pretentions to goodness. A troublesome mule can easily be substituted in this example:

There was an old Quaker farmer who had a very bad-tempered cow. Every time he sat down to milk her, she'd cause trouble—slap him in the face with her tail, kick over the milk bucket, and generally make milking time miserable. One day things were especially bad, with the cow kicking bucket, stool, and Quaker himself into a heap on the barn floor. Enough was enough, even for a peaceable Quaker. "Nay, bossy," said the farmer as he dusted himself off, "thee knows that I cannot strike thee, but on the morrow I'll sell you to the Baptist down the road, and he'll beat the tar out of thee."

In contrast, here is a Quaker in-joke based on the sense that sometimes a common theme or message many be hovering over an entire silent meeting:

Near the end of a long and very silent meeting for worship, one Friend finally rose and spoke. After meeting he turned to the Friend who had been sitting silently next to him and said, "Next time speak for thyself."

QUAKERS IN BUSINESS AND SCIENCE

In the west of England an iron bridge spans the gorge of the Severn River on a single graceful arch. The builder was Quaker Abraham Darby, whose family ironworks at nearby Coalbrookdale fabricated nearly 1700 structural members and pieced them together in 1779. The world's first bridge to be built from iron is now the focus of a UNESCO World Heritage Site. It is a monument to the industrial transformation of Britain, and also a memorial to the role of Quakers in industrial change. Darby's grandfather (also

Abraham) innovated in iron smelting, gaining a reputation for lightweight pots and kettles, and building a substantial industrial community in the Severn Valley. Many other Quakers were active in early metal industries, being responsible for two-thirds of the British iron business in the first decades of the eighteenth century, developing new products and processes, building machinery, and eventually building the first iron-railed railway from Stockton to Darlington in 1825—known as "the Quaker Railroad."

Twenty-first-century Quakers are more likely to be teachers or physicians than factory owners, but industry and science have long been prominent. Quakerism from the start was solidly practical, emphasizing personal experience over abstract ideas. George Fox himself talked about knowing the divine spirit "experimentally," by which he meant through direct personal experience. Building Quaker meetings in the face of religious restrictions and knitting them together into a movement was hands-on work. Added to this orientation was British law that reserved university education for members of the Church of England until 1871. This meant that Quakers could not train for careers in law or medicine or serve in government jobs. At this time the British economy was in the midst of revolutionary growth and technological change with steam power and factory production. Ambitious young men who wanted more to life than farming turned to private enterprise.

Quakerism's rejection of appeals to authority and official wisdom was also compatible with the emerging nexus of scientific inquiry. British chemist John Dalton and American naturalist John Bartram were among the notable Quaker scientists. Astronomer Maria Mitchell was the first woman elected to the American Academy of Arts and Sciences and the first woman to be accepted into the American Philosophical Society, although her Quaker meeting ousted her for owning a piano. By one calculation, the Royal Society, the leading British scientific organization, accepted vastly more Friends than would be expected from their share of the British population during the second half of the nineteenth century.

The Quaker reputation for integrity also promoted business success. Early Friends were known for selling goods at a fixed price rather than bargaining, making them attractive and reliable business partners. Commerce in the eighteenth-century Atlantic world revolved around family networks in which different family members might be based in London or Bristol, Philadelphia, the Caribbean, and Europe, exchanging information and handling sales and purchases. The trustworthiness of Quakers allowed them to participate in networks that extended beyond direct family ties. This network effect was particularly important in finance, where Quakers were the founders of both the Barclays and Lloyds banks—the former dating from 1690 and growing by merging with other Quaker banking enterprises, the latter founded in 1765.

In the United States, Quakers were similarly innovators in retailing, founding two of the country's most prominent department stores. R.H. Macy, from a Quaker whaling family on Nantucket Island, opened his New York dry goods store in 1858. A decade later, Justus Strawbridge and Isaac Clothier cooperated across the Orthodox–Hicksite divide to open Philadelphia's most prominent department store in 1868.

Family ties and other Quaker connections facilitated concentration in industries beyond iron, steel, and metallurgy. British Quakers fed the world's sweet tooth. The Fry family in Bristol, the Rowntrees in York, and the Cadbury family in Birmingham developed techniques for turning bitter cacao from West Africa into smooth milk chocolate and dominated British chocolate manufacturing. Cadbury sold more chocolate worldwide than any other firm by the mid-twentieth century. New England Quakers dominated the whaling ports of New Bedford and Nantucket during the first half of the nineteenth century when whale oil was the preferred fuel for lamps. Herman Melville's great whaling novel *Moby-Dick* features the "Quaker ship" *Pequod*, owned by Peleg and Bildad, irascible retired ship captains, and held to course by its upright chief mate Starbuck.

Business success carried problems. How could you reconcile great wealth with plainness and simplicity? The easiest solution, in both Britain and America, was to opt in favor of enjoying one's money by leaving the Society of Friends for the Church of England or the Episcopalians. Others managed to reconcile the tension. George Cadbury built a giant corporation and bought himself very nice houses, but he also created a model community for the workers at his factory in Bournville on the south side of Birmingham. Houses were available at prices that skilled workers and technicians could afford. He wanted to control how the community developed, but did not see it as a source of profit or means for controlling workers. Toward the end of his life he transferred most of his assets to the Bournville Village Trust that continues to support the charming neighborhood and other good works. His first large estate became the Woodbrooke Quaker study center. Joseph Rowntree took similar steps on a smaller scale. Someone looking at Cadbury or Rowntree through twenty-first-century eyes might dismiss their philanthropy as superficial, but we should contrast them instead with industrialists who were their contemporaries, like the sanctimonious and rapacious George Pullman, whose "model town" south of Chicago bred bitter labor violence.

The moral dilemmas would be more intractable. In 1795, Birmingham Monthly Meeting in England disowned Samuel Galton, Jr. for continuing to manufacture guns. Galton was shocked, because his family had been manufacturing firearms for decades, and he complained that he was singled out when people who made buttons for military uniforms or boxes for cartridges were ignored. It was a version of the modern question of socially responsible investing, when lists of unwanted companies have very fuzzy edges. Perhaps you don't want to invest in fossil fuels, but what about a petroleum company that is expanding its research in renewables? Should you eliminate all businesses that have any military contracts or just those where the military is a major customer? In Galton's case, Friends had originally treated guns as tools used by farmers and hunters. The expanding scale of warfare leading to the Napoleonic Wars changed their thinking. In 1742, Quakers asked each other: "Do you bear a faithful and Christian testimony against the receiving or paying tithes? And against bearing arms?" Over the decades, the query became stronger and more pointed, and Friends began to highlight the role of guns and the gun trade in propagating slavery. By 1795, the revulsion against slavery and against mass warfare left Galton on the outside.

Slavery of a different sort also blindsided the Cadburys. In 1901, they were informed that the cocoa they were buying from Portuguese colonies in Africa was grown by Africans who were effectively slaves. It was a bit like having an investigative reporter reveal that one of today's big shoe companies used overseas suppliers with a terrible human rights record. The Cadburys sent investigators and tried to work with the British and Portuguese governments, but the impact was small and they kept buying on the theory that a boycott by a single company would not make a difference. The choice to work on the "inside" to make change rather than taking a public stand opened them to charges of hypocrisy and a blaring accusation by the *Standard* newspaper. Cadbury Ltd. sued the paper for libel and won, but they had been embarrassed by a dilemma of international business that was especially painful for a company that tried to live by Quaker principles.

BOX 3.4   HERMAN MELVILLE'S CYNICAL TAKE ON QUAKERS IN BUSINESS

In the early pages of *Moby-Dick*, the narrator Ishmael has decided to go whaling and visits the *Pequod*, where he meets its owners Captain Peleg and Captain Bildad. Before the chapter is over, the two have played a good cop–bad cop routine and flummoxed Ishmael into accepting lower wages than he intends or deserves. Here is how he describes coming on board to find Peleg, who then takes him to meet the co-owner:

> There was nothing so very particular, perhaps, about the appearance of the elderly man I saw; he was brown and brawny, like most old seamen, and heavily rolled up in blue pilot-cloth, cut in the Quaker style; only there was a fine and almost microscopic net-work of the minutest wrinkles interlacing round his eyes, which must have arisen from his continual sailings in many hard gales, and always looking to windward;—for this causes the muscles about the eyes to become pursed together. Such eye-wrinkles are very effectual in a scowl ...

> I saw ... this old seaman, as an insulated Quakerish Nantucketer, was full of his insular prejudices, and rather distrustful of all aliens, unless they hailed from Cape Cod or the Vineyard ...

Seated on the transom was what seemed to me a most uncommon and surprising figure. It turned out to be Captain Bildad, who along with Captain Peleg was one of the largest owners of the vessel; the other shares, as is sometimes the case in these ports, being held by a crowd of old annuitants; widows, fatherless children, and chancery wards; each owning about the value of a foot of plank or ... nail or two in the ship ...

Now, Bildad, like Peleg, and indeed many other Nantucketers, was a Quaker, the island having been originally settled by that sect; and to this day its inhabitants in general retain in an uncommon measure the peculiarities of the Quaker, only variously and anomalously modified by things altogether alien and heterogeneous. For some of these same Quakers are the most sanguinary of all sailors and whale-hunters. They are fighting Quakers; they are Quakers with a vengeance.

Like Captain Peleg, Captain Bildad was a well-to-do, retired whaleman. But unlike Captain Peleg—who cared not a rush for what are called serious things, and indeed deemed those self-same serious things the veriest of all trifles—Captain Bildad had not only been originally educated according to the strictest sect of Nantucket Quakerism, but all his subsequent ocean life, and the sight of many unclad, lovely island creatures, round the Horn—all that had not moved this native born Quaker one single jot, had not so much as altered one angle of his vest ... Though refusing, from conscientious scruples, to bear arms against land invaders, yet himself had illimitably invaded the Atlantic and Pacific; and though a sworn foe to human bloodshed, yet had he in his straight-bodied coat, spilled tuns upon tuns of leviathan gore. How now in the contemplative evening of his days, the pious Bildad reconciled these things in the reminiscence, I do not know; but it did not seem to concern him much, and very probably he had long since come to the sage and sensible conclusion that a man's religion is one thing, and this practical world quite another.

QUAKERS AND SOCIAL BETTERMENT

Nineteenth-century Friends were an important source of social reform energy. They sparked social betterment movements that grew beyond the Society of Friends. Individuals from all branches were leaders in advocating the abolition of slavery and assisting the Underground Railroad before the Civil War, in the campaign for women's rights, and in providing education and other opportunities for freed slaves. They were active in the temperance movement and in advocacy for Native Americans. Friends were also visible in the relief work and peace advocacy which eventually took new shape in the creation of the American Friends Service Committee (AFSC) and many other similar organizations.

Lucretia Mott was a gentle Quaker powerhouse whose activism touched many of these essential reforms. She traveled in the ministry, lectured wherever she could find an audience, and organized people for action. In 1833 she helped to create the Philadelphia Female Anti-Slavery Society—interracial and interdenominational but limited to one gender by social conventions. She took on peace advocacy, temperance, and the needs of Native American women in her spare time. She went as a delegate to the World Anti-Slavery Convention in London in 1840, only to be rebuffed because only men were to be seated. The experience led her to develop plans for a women's rights meeting. Working with several other Quaker women and with Elizabeth Cady Stanton, her idea culminated in what became the Seneca Falls Convention in 1848, the landmark declaration of the equal rights of women. One of the speakers was Amy Post, a friend of African American abolitionist Frederick Douglas, a Progressive Friend on the radical margin of Quakerism, and one of Marge's distant relatives. Mott would continue tireless work for women's rights and was joined in leadership by the younger Quaker Susan B. Anthony.

In Britain Elizabeth Fry took the lead in trying to improve the horrible conditions for imprisoned women and children, a cause soon taken up in the United States. She grew up in a well-connected Quaker family, the sister of Joseph John Gurney. In her early thirties she discovered her own gift for ministry. In 1813 she first visited women and children held in Newgate prison, bringing clothing, food, and necessities. She also began a school for women prisoners that taught the Bible to women who were often illiterate along with practical knitting and needlework. A related cause was work to better the conditions for women who were being shipped to Australia as convicts. Her work to organize other middle-class women and her lobbying of influential men helped to push England to take first steps to humanize its dreadful prison system.

Women's rights and recognition was also important in the Quaker missionary message. The school for girls that Friends established in Ramallah, Palestine in 1869 has thrived and grown for a century and a half, expanding to include boys in 1901. Quaker recognition of the spiritual gifts of women also promoted gender equality in daily life. For instance, Kenyan women challenged the traditional belief that women who ate chicken could not bear healthy children. Thus, eating eggs and chicken became a mark of faith for Luhya women—a small manifestation of significant changes. More importantly, women were educated and eventually began to be accepted as preachers and clerks in most every land Quakers reached.

As Americans struggled over the future of slavery, growing demands for its immediate and absolute abolition raised dilemmas. Quakers had rid themselves of slave-holding as individuals and as a religious society, but well-settled meetings were not always happy when traveling ministers arrived with calls for radical uprooting of slavery in the South. At the same time, many Friends in the Northern states actively aided escaping slaves through the informal networks of free Northern Blacks and white supporters who provided safe houses and transportation for what has become known as the Underground Railroad. The blockbuster novel *Uncle Tom's Cabin* (1852) has a chapter in which the fugitive slaves Eliza and George Harris shelter on a Quaker farm in Ohio on their escape to Canada. The American Civil War compounded the problem. Some Friends thought that the righteousness of the Union cause justified taking up arms, while others remained steadfast against joining in the war—a dilemma at the center of the novel and film *Friendly Persuasion.*

BOX 3.5   JOHN GREENLEAF WHITTIER: QUAKER POET AND ABOLITIONIST

During the COVID-19 lockdown in 2020, many Americans revisited "Snow-Bound," John Greenleaf Whittier's long poem about a New England family waiting out a blizzard by sharing stories at the fireside. Whittier (1807–96) grew up in a Quaker family and remained a Quaker through his life. He was a popular poet and one of the founders of the *Atlantic Monthly* literary magazine. He was also an unrelenting abolitionist who was a founder of the American Anti-Slavery Society in 1833. He edited a series of abolitionist newspapers from 1828 until 1857, calling for immediate emancipation at some peril to himself, and published anti-slavery poems. He was a Quaker activist who was deeply engaged in politics, working to persuade sympathetic Congressmen to stand up for their principles. He helped to organize the Liberty Party in 1839 and then the Free Soil Party, some of the seeds from which the anti-slavery Republican Party of Abraham Lincoln would grow. Later in life he mentored several successful women writers. Today he is best known for the patriotic Civil War poem "Barbara Frietchie" that was once a staple of school literature classes in the United States ("Shoot if you must, this old gray head / But spare my country's flag," she said), for the hymn "Dear Lord and Father of Mankind," and for the often misquoted lines from his poem "Maud Muller" ("For of all sad words of tongue or pen, / The saddest are these: 'It might have been!'"). Whittier, California, birthplace of US President Richard Nixon, was founded as a Quaker community.

Activist women did not have an easy time. Quakers had long recognized women's spiritual gifts for ministry, but social norms precluded them speaking to public gatherings that were judged "promiscuous," meaning men and women in the same audience. The solution was often to speak in someone's parlor or from their front porch. Quakers may have abhorred slavery, but Quaker men could be very uncomfortable when the message was carried by fierce women such as Angelina Grimké or Abby Kelley Foster, who left the Society of Friends because stodgy and cautious meetings often refused to open meetinghouses to anti-slavery speakers.

Other types of social activism raised similar questions about how to participate with larger social causes or government programs while remaining true to Quaker principles. Friends had a long-standing interest in fair dealing with Native Americans. They had been unusual in the colonies in their concern for the Native rights. They organized the Friendly Association for Regaining and Preserving Peace with the Indians by Pacific Measures in 1756. A century later, when President Grant implemented a "Peace Policy" for relations with Native Americans in 1869, he asked Quakers to serve as Indian Agents (government representatives and supervisors) for several tribes in Oklahoma, Kansas, and Nebraska. The Friends who accepted were certainly an improvement on many federal Indian Agents who were often corrupt and contemptuous of the people they were supposed to help. At the same time, good Quaker intentions could not mask the fact that they were operating within a system that devalued tribal cultures and independence, and many Quakers participated in staffing the boarding schools for Native Americans that are now considered a tragic mistake for weakening families and undermining tribal culture.

British Friends took up the causes of temperance, economic justice, and peace. John Bright was the second Quaker elected to Parliament after repeal of the Test Act opened elective office to dissenting Protestants and Catholics. He successfully campaigned for the 1846 repeal of the Corn Laws that prevented the export of English grain to relieve the Irish Famine. He led the Peace Society and with many other Friends opposed the Crimean War of 1854–6, which wasted men and money for an abstract notion of power politics. His influence helped keep Britain from supporting slave states in the Civil War. Nevertheless, some more conservative Friends were fearful that participating fully in government in pursuit of good ends required too much compromise of beliefs, a choice that bedevils some Friends to the present day.

DIVERGENT PATHS

Richmond, Indiana and Manchester, England were vastly different places in the late nineteenth century. Richmond was a small, quiet community of fewer than 20,000 people with a modest main street, square frame houses, and a few fancier brick mansions for bankers and merchants. It served the needs of the prosperous farms that surrounded it, many owned by Quaker families who had settled the area early in the century. Manchester was Britain's leading industrial powerhouse, a sprawling city of smoke-spewing factories, technological innovation, and extremes of wealth and poverty that had inspired some of the most powerful depictions of the industrial revolution. It could have swallowed Richmond 40 times over.

We draw the contrast because two important gatherings summed up the developing differences within the Society of Friends and pointed the way to key developments in the twentieth century. In 1887, Indiana Yearly Meeting called for Gurneyite meetings to send delegates to Richmond to debate the acceptability of water baptism as practiced by other evangelicals. Although most yearly meetings had rejected the practice before the meeting opened, the conference turned into a larger deliberation about the defining characteristics of these more evangelical meetings. The result was the Richmond Declaration of Faith, a long document intended to hold the Society of Friends together around a common understanding of fundamental doctrine.

The Richmond Declaration is a hybrid. The first half is a set of assertions about God, Christ, the Bible, resurrection and atonement, and other Christian basics that a contemporary Methodist or Presbyterian would have endorsed. At the same time, it maintains some of the core Quaker beliefs about simplicity, oaths, peace, and sacraments. A number of evangelical yearly meetings, especially those influenced by the holiness movement, embraced the Declaration as a statement of faith, and it remains an important reference point for many Friends.

Where the Richmond gathering reinforced evangelical Quakerism, a conference in Manchester in 1895 challenged it. With traditional Christianity under pressure from scientific discoveries and historical research about the origins of the Bible, younger British Friends wanted to explore ways to bring Quakerism more in line with modern understandings of the world—appropriately in a city that was doing so much to upend traditional England. Although London Yearly Meeting did not accept the Manchester report, it was an important step in liberalizing the Society. It was a key step in the broader move toward religious modernism among both Hicksites and those Orthodox Friends who were not part of the Holiness movement. Quaker modernism accepted the centrality of continuing and direct revelation, saw modern biblical scholarship as a continuation of the Quaker past, and endorsed the broader Social Gospel movement—all ideas that resonate with liberal Quakers in the twenty-first century.

NOTE

1 Other Quaker colleges that date from the nineteenth century are Guilford (North Carolina), Wilmington (Ohio), Earlham (Indiana), William Penn (Iowa), and George Fox (Oregon).

FURTHER READING

Margaret Hope Bacon, *Mothers of Feminism: The Story of Quaker Women in America* (New York: Harper & Row, 1986). An introduction to Quaker women in the forefront of social change, from Lucretia Mott and Susan B. Anthony into the twentieth century with Alice Paul and others.

Deborah Cadbury, *Chocolate Wars: The 150-Year Rivalry between the World's Greatest Chocolate Makers* (New York: Public Affairs, 2010). How Quaker families dealt with the challenges and responsibilities of business success.

Thomas D. Hamm, *The Transformation of American Quakerism* (Bloomington, IN: Indiana University Press, 1988). The authoritative source on the effects of westward movement on American Quakers.

Hannah Whitall Smith, *The Christian's Secret of a Happy Life* (Grand Rapids, MI: Revell, 2012). A devotional classic originally published in 1875 that has sold millions of copies and greatly influenced evangelical Friends.

John Woolman, *The Journal of John Woolman* (available in many editions). The single most influential writing by an American Quaker. Woolman's many writings are analyzed and summarized in Michael Birkel, *A Near Sympathy: The Timeless Quaker Wisdom of John Woolman* (Richmond, IN: Friends United Press, 2010).

A WORLDWIDE FAITH IN THE TWENTIETH CENTURY AND BEYOND

> For more than a hundred years, a continuous stream of traveling ministers went forth from one end of the Society of Friends to the other, formulating the message of Friends, awakening the youth, maintaining the unity of the loosely formed body, convincing new persons to join in membership, and convicting existing members to become ministers.
>
> (Baker and Makhino 2009, p, 5)

The United Society of Friends Women formed in the late 1800s as Quaker women in the United States learned about their mutual passion for mission work. As Priscilla Makhino and Marian Baker noted in 2009, "more recently Friends of Bolivia have traveled to share the good news into Peru and Inuit [Eskimo] Quakers from Alaska have crossed the Bering Strait to share Christ with their distant relatives in Siberia." Kenyans travel far from their homes "due to a calling of Gospel love, not due to a specific concern" (Baker and Makhino 2009, p. 5).

Makhino and Baker are among the many Friends who are working to revitalize the practice of traveling in the ministry. Visiting among Friends has been crucial in spreading Quaker theology and practice for nearly four hundred years, not just the first century referenced in the opening quotation. The minimal structure of Quaker meetings and the absence of an overriding institutional authority required Friends to rely on the informal connections and relationships built by individual ministers who might travel for months at a time and for hundreds or even thousands of miles. Traveling ministers, also known as public Friends, carried letters indicating the support of their home meetings. They brought news and often shared inspiring words during worship. They often visited each family in a community in their homes, offering worshipful support, or spoke at open meetings for non-Friends as well as local Quakers.

This travel in the ministry is a time-honored practice among Friends. George Fox himself traveled to the Caribbean and North America. A century and a half later, for one example, British Friends began mission work in Madagascar in 1818, developing a vigorous indigenous church before meeting resistance from the Malagasy queen. Invited back in 1861, the British missionaries were surprised to find the church had flourished. Joseph Sewell, a British educator and recorded minister left his own motherless children in order to take up this work. Ambohijatavo school quickly became a leading boys' school in the capital city, and Helen Gilpin successfully established Umpadrana girls' school. Friends soon were overseeing education of over 12,000 students. The schools remain as evidence of this early Quaker presence.

The sometimes unexpected connections possible through travel in the ministry have offered an alternative to mission work, separate from the colonial biases that have often gone side-by-side with missions. Individual ministers arrive at established or nascent Quaker communities and spend a few days or perhaps weeks, strengthening the local bodies and helping them better thrive. But they do not establish a church which would then be dependent on further mission work for years or decades as often in the nineteenth and twentieth centuries.

This chapter summarizes the extent of Quakerism in the early twenty-first century and then works its way around the world from Africa to Latin America, Asia and the Pacific, Europe, and finally to North America. At each stop we trace the twentieth-century expansion of the Religious Society of Friends in different parts of the world and describe the distinctive ways in which Quakerism has developed in different cultural contexts.

Table 4.1 Key dates for Quakerism from 1900

1900	Friends General Conference (FGC) established.
1902	Missionaries arrive in Chiquimula, Guatemala.
1902	Five Years Meeting (renamed Friends United Meeting (FUM) in 1965) established.
1903	Friends United Meeting sends missionaries to East Africa.
1914	War Victims' Relief Committee established by British Friends. Friends Ambulance Unit created to provide care for soldiers and civilians injured in World War I.
1917	American Friends Service Committee (AFSC) established.
1920	First All Friends Conference publishes *Friends and War*
1928	British Friends Service Council established by London and Ireland yearly meetings
1937	Second World Conference of Friends held in Swarthmore, Pennsylvania. Friends World Committee for Consultation (FWCC) founded.
1946	East Africa Yearly Meeting formed, the first such body in Africa.
1947	Nobel Peace Prize awarded to AFSC and Friends Service Council (Britain) on behalf of the Religious Society of Friends.
1950	Friends Theological College established in Kaimosi, Kenya
1955	Meetings divided by 1827 separation rejoin, forming united yearly meetings in New York, Canada, and Philadelphia.
1965	Establishment of Evangelical Friends Alliance (becoming Evangelical Friends International (EFI) in 1994).
1970	Evangelical Friends Church in Guatemala established as an independent body.
1974	Bolivian Friends Yearly Meeting established.
1985	First World Gathering of Young Friends held at Guilford College, North Carolina.
1990	First International Theological Conference of Quaker Women held at Woodbrooke Quaker Study Centre in England.
1991	Fifth World Conference of Friends held at venues in Kenya, the Netherlands, and Honduras.
1999	Evangelical Friends International-Africa Region opens the Great Lakes School of Theology at Bujumbura, Burundi.
2009	Kaimosi Friends University College opens in Kenya.
2010s	Separations in Indiana, North Carolina, and Northwest yearly meetings.
2012	Sixth World Gathering of Friends in Kenya.
2016	Friends World Committee Plenary in Peru.

TWENTY-FIRST-CENTURY QUAKERISM

Friends in the twenty-first century are present on every inhabited continent, with the largest concentrations in East Africa, Britain, the United States, and several nations in Central and South America. The separations among Friends in North America that began in 1827, some of which remain as of this writing, spread into the rest of the world through mission work and peace and justice efforts. East African Friends have been linked with Friends United Meeting (FUM) based in Richmond, Indiana. Friends in the African Great Lakes Region of Rwanda and Burundi have longstanding ties with Evangelical Friends Church International (EFCI). Most Asian Friends also relate to EFCI, although Japan Yearly Meeting has strong British and Philadelphia connections, particularly since World War II when Elizabeth Grey Vining served as tutor to the crown prince.[1] At best count, 49 percent of the approximately 378,000 Quakers in 2017 lived in Africa, 22 percent in North America, 14 percent in the Caribbean and Latin America, 9 percent in Europe and the Middle East, and 6 percent in the Asia and the western Pacific region.[2]

FRIENDS IN EAST AFRICA: FROM MISSION FIELD TO SELF-SUSTAINING DENOMINATIONS

African Friends grew from 157,000 members in 2007 to 181,400 a decade later. Almost all African yearly meetings originated from

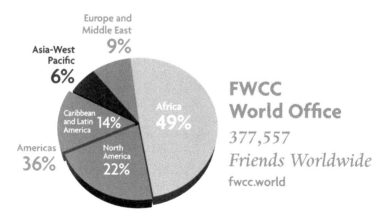

Figure 4.1 Friends around the world, 2017 (Friends World Committee for Consultation)

Table 4.2 Changing shares of Friends around the world: percentage of total

	1950	2017
Africa	13	49
North America	70	22
Latin America	4	14
Europe and Middle East	12	9
Asia and West Pacific	1	6

missionary work by North Americans and participate in either Friends United Meeting (FUM) or Evangelical Friends Church International (EFCI). A notable exception is South Africa, where an unprogrammed yearly meeting dates to 1948. As of 2020, at least 120,000 Friends, and perhaps many more, are part of the 19 yearly meetings in Kenya, two yearly meetings in Tanzania, and one in Uganda that affiliate with FUM. Another 47,600 Quakers in Burundi and 6,000 in Rwanda are in yearly meetings that relate to EFCI.

Western Kenya, although near the equator, has a moderate climate due to its high altitude. Rains and good soil that make it an important agricultural area contributed to its selection by American Quaker missionaries in 1902 as the base for the Friends Africa Industrial Mission. Friends set for themselves the goal of converting the Luhya (or Luyia) people by their fourfold ministry of evangelism, education, industrial training, and medical work. Daudi Lung'aho encountered American missionaries Willis Hotchkiss, Edgar Hole, and Arthur Chilson near Kaimosi soon after their arrival, and his heart was drawn to their work, as was that of Maria Maraga. She soon married Lung'aho and became counselor to staff and students at the Girls School the missionaries had established. Others joined them and by 1903 about 50 people were connected to the mission station. The Protestant denominations that worked in the British colony of Kenya agreed in 1907 to concentrate in different areas or "spheres of influence" and confirmed western Kenya for Quaker work (declaring spheres of influence was a very colonialist practice, of course).

Esther Mombo of Highlands Yearly Meeting is a Kenyan Quaker scholar who has studied the complications missionaries faced in transplanting Midwestern American Quaker practice into the Luhya culture. She notes how traditional, tribal practices such as prohibition on women eating chicken (it was considered to create infertility), "bridewealth," and polygamy became the focus of mission efforts for women's equality. However, while eating chicken soon became a mark of Quaker women, not all efforts had the desired effect.

> The treatment of polygamy as a moral issue had negative implications on women. First, it failed to address the issue of inequality between men and women in the Luyia society. Second, and more important, it created untold misery for the women who were evicted from poly-gamy, as no one would support them. These women became single mothers in a society where polygamy was designed to cater for them as wives but not as single mothers ... By denouncing the traditional customs which defined the role and place of women, Quaker mis-sionaries set out to restructure the gender roles in the society and replace them with Victorian ideals of womanhood which stressed domesticity and female subordination.
>
> (Mombo 1999, p. 7)

Despite inadequate understandings of local culture, the missions were a place where women gained skills and respect. Women formed prayer groups at each of the mission stations. As they have done in many other places, Quakers established schools, especially for girls. Just as education for the men became a path for Kenyans to become clerks of local meetings, the educated women were instrumental in forming their own separate meetings. The Women's Yearly Meeting, established in 1952, developed organi-zational and leadership skills among East African women. Later the United Society of Friends Women Kenya (USFWK) connected the women as multiple yearly meetings formed.

Kenyan Quakers have continued to put faith into action through schools for both boys and girls. Joel Litu and other Friends translated the Bible into Luragoli. Spoken in western Kenya, it is one of that nation's many languages. The Bible has been used as a school textbook, as literacy and Christianity were considered inse-parable. Kenyan Friends have sponsored more than 1,200 schools in Kenya, although teachers and administration at these schools are now public employees who focus on student mastery of nationally mandated standards. However, many village meetings retain close ties with their local schools. As is true in much of the world, education for girls and concern for changing women's roles in society characterizes Kenyan Quaker schools.

Friends Bible Institute, founded in 1942, now Friends Theological College, trains both women and men as pastors. It was originally under the care of East Africa Yearly Meeting. Friends United Meeting took responsibility in the 1990s at the request of the yearly meeting in acknowledgement of its importance for all African Friends. Friends Teachers Training College in Kaimosi operates as a government school but with Quaker sponsorship.

In Kenya and elsewhere in Africa, Friends experienced pressure from other Christians over beliefs necessary for membership. Membership requires completion of a substantial adult curriculum known as Book 1 and Book 2. Kenyans generally have accepted theological explanations about Quaker understandings of membership and baptism by the Holy Spirit. East Africa Yearly Meeting (EAYM) was established and became self-governing in 1946, retaining affiliation with Friends United Meeting. In 1958 Thomas Lung'aho became the first administrative secretary of EAYM although Americans continued to supervise much of the work of the mission. Even though women had done much to support its formation, including raising needed funds, they were left out of the leadership of this body. In 1951 women formed their own yearly meeting. Only in 1964, a year after Kenyan independence, did East Africa Yearly Meeting gain responsibility for all its property and projects. It comprised diverse tribes in what has been called the Luhya super-tribal group. As the number of Friends in Kenya increased, other yearly meetings formed through divisions that began in 1979 with the Bukusu group separating to form Elgon Religious Society of Friends. This was the first of several schisms, often along tribal lines.

During the struggle for Kenyan independence in the 1950s and 1960s, Kenyan Quakers established Friends Center at the Ofafa housing estate in Nairobi with the initial goal of feeding detainees from detention camps. They also established a similar center in Mwea Central Province north of Nairobi. Both soon provided social, educational, and health services, and served as community centers and Friends meeting houses. After independence, they also did pioneering work in agricultural and industrial development at a time when the government was settling thousands of people on land formerly owned by Europeans. Beginning in the 1960s the Women's Yearly Meeting took up prison ministry now carried on by USFWK. These women, with little formal training or expectation of pay, would share their knowledge of the Bible, much as Elizabeth Fry had done in English prisons two centuries earlier. They were convinced that even if society condemned these prisoners, God would forgive them. Friends' influence extended to Jomo Kenyatta, the first post-colonial president of Kenya, who spent a term at the Quaker Woodbrooke College in England in the 1930s.

In the twenty-first century, concern for reconciliation and healing has required many individuals to step out of their comfort zones to rebuild trust and community. Mombo and Nyiramana (2016, p. 10) speak to Friends' understanding of peacebuilding in words that echo as prophetic in a time when nations worldwide are rejecting people because of their ethnicity, religion, or nationality:

> An important aim of our peacebuilding has been to help communities to heal and be reconciled to each other so that they grow together as communities. Violence causes segregation along identity lines, with individuals and groups becoming isolated and exclusive, claiming that they are only safe "when with my people." As Quakers we embark on peacebuilding to help reconcile people to God, to their neighbors and to nature. Our work begins with dealing with the hurt at the individual level, and also healing at all levels of society for lasting peace. We do this because conflict in our region is rooted in a politics of exclusion in which people find themselves denied their identity, freedom or resources ... the first step is forgiveness ... healing past hurts and framing a vision for a better future.

National Quaker bodies now work alongside FUM and link across the several yearly meetings. United Society of Friends Women Kenya encourages a common mission and vision and connects Kenyans with women from the United States. They began to hold women's prayer days in 1990, a practice that in recent years has gathered upward of 4,000 Quaker women every three months for a day of prayer. They held their first triennial meeting in 1996. The United Society of Friends Women International met in Kenya for the first time in 2010. Friends Church in Kenya (FCK) organized in 1987 to promote cooperation among all the yearly meetings in the region and to serve as Friends' liaison with the National Council of Churches in Kenya.

Young adults who had participated in the World Gathering of Young Friends in Greensboro, North Carolina in 1985 established the third coordinating body in East Africa, Kenyan Young Friends, with the assistance of Friends World Committee for Consultation (see Chapters 1 and 7). These Friends retain connections with others from around the world and are a bridge between generations. They have encouraged lively music and charismatic styles including speaking in tongues that are rejected by their elders. Along with organizational efforts, they have sought to encourage work to protect the environment.

Despite the long connection with Friends United Meeting, FUM held its Triennial Meeting for the first time in Kenya in 2002. That year a group mainly of Kenyans and a few North Americans wrote *Christian Faith and Practice in the Friends Church*, published in both English and Swahili. FUM was scheduled to meet again in Kenya in 2020 before the COVID-19 pandemic intervened.

Post-colonial self-determination remains a significant issue for many East African Friends. Some question their relationship with FUM, which continues to provide significant financial and practical support. For other Kenyans, participation in the international FUM is an important part of their personal identity and a heritage on which they draw. In this context, they are increasingly working to reset the balance between the need for outside funds to undertake work, whether construction of new churches or underwriting peacebuilding and reconciliation work, and the importance of local control. Awareness that donors may not understand local dynamics or be interested in cooperating with local structures has led African recipients of international aid to work hard to ensure that such funds are not exacerbating the problems. Kenyans are aware that the after-effects of violence can be used to justify external agendas and create new situations of dependency. Mombo and Nyiramana advocate for sustainable peacebuilding grounded in a holistic approach to conflict that addresses local political as well as spiritual and ethnic issues and includes all stakeholders, especially women. The needs of local communities must be at the core of action (2016, pp. 34, 35).

Kenyan worship has evolved in its own ways. For many years, meetings might fill Sunday with three different gatherings, a first meeting with singing, prayers, and a homily, a second meeting for business and worship, and an afternoon meeting to ensure people were living what they were taught. In the afternoon men and women met separately to allow freer sharing. Gradually mid-week meetings for women formed. At these *Haramisi* (Thursday) and *Jumaa* (Friday) meetings women practiced organizing skills and supported one another through prayer, gaining skills needed to read the Bible. Miriam Were, plenary speaker at the 1991 World Conference of Friends, noted one of the consequences of this attention to everyday life—that Quaker villages were where men did not drink or beat their wives and children.

Quaker Christianity in Kenya has been influenced by both African traditional religion and the broader global culture. Worship time is fluid, full of song, Bible reading, preaching, and prayer, which may be in a local dialect, in English, or in Swahili. Some Friends, such as the Samburu, include lively dance. The presiding clerk rather than the pastor may take the lead, although this varies from meeting to meeting. Over the years, as literacy has spread, the focus has shifted from a storytelling approach to reading, although pastors note the importance of story in helping people remember what they have been taught. Vocal prayer and speaking directly to God resonate with African religious traditions. Members of the congregation may seek attention and support from God, ask others to support them, or seek a pastor to be a mediator with God. Occasionally Friends organize *Keshas*—overnight prayer meetings for spiritual and emotional refreshment. Prayer and worship songs are lively and energetic, and may also include times of unprogrammed simultaneous personal vocal prayer.

Marge attended worship several times in Kenya while attending the World Conference of Friends in 1991. At the worship in

Nairobi that she first attended, she arrived with her host (a well-known woman evangelist who was immediately consulted about who was preaching) to find a group standing in the front of the community center where they met. A young couple had just lost a child. Each person in the group spoke. Singing followed. After Marge was introduced, the singing continued. Several other groups used the building for worship so the sound of drums permeated the whole building, an interesting counterpoint to the Quaker choir, along with calls to prayer from the mosque across the street. At other worship services either her host or one of the foreigners who came for the World Conference spoke. Who was to speak seemed to be determined by the evangelist consulting with the clerk after their arrival. Another time, a local politician spoke to the importance of the church in maintaining peace and stability in Kenya. This was followed by a request from a member of the congregation for federal support in building a new church, noting that Quakers don't criticize the government. Marge had to laugh when one Kenyan Friend whispered to her as they left worship at the Conference that many Kenyans are bored with so little singing and preaching and so much silence.

Not surprisingly, some younger Friends prefer electronic keyboards, microphones, and praise dancing and song, unlike older members who often insist on slow hymns and traditional sermon styles. Modern technology allows individuals to follow church services on television or engage in video conferences. Cell phones are common and much communication does not require face-to-face meetings in contrast to traditional expectations of personal connections. The result has been a loss of younger Friends to other denominations, although some Friends churches have adopted the new ways (a phenomenon not confined to African Friends).

In recent decades, Kenyan missionaries have reached out to form churches among the pastoral Samburu people of the north-central Rift Valley of Kenya, where their message has been especially appealing to women. Other outreach has occurred in the Congo, Tanzania, and South Sudan. Kenyan Friends have grown from being a "mission-receiving" church to being "mission-sending" bodies, a change which marks increasing maturity as part of the wider Christian community.

THE GREAT LAKES REGION OF CENTRAL AFRICA: HEALING AND RECONCILIATION

Life in the former Belgian colonies of Rwanda, Burundi, and the Democratic Republic of the Congo has been sorely tested by ongoing violence between Hutus and Tutsis culminating the 1994 genocide when over a million people died.

Arthur and Edna Chilson, two of the first missionaries in Kenya, were advocates of the revivals associated with Holy Spirit movement in Kenya. The Board of Friends Africa Mission did not return them to Kenya after a furlough in the United States. Consequently, the Chilsons founded the Evangelical Friends Church in Burundi, to be run on more evangelical theology, in line with Evangelical Friends International. After Burundi expelled foreign missionaries in 1980, Burundians formed Église Évangélique des Amis du Burundi in 1984.

Quakers soon reached out to open churches in the Congo and also in Rwanda in 1987. The Communaute des Eglise Evangelique au Congo (Community of Evangelical Church of Congo) includes most Friends in the country. They are evangelical, programmed Friends affiliated with Burundi Yearly Meeting. A small group of about 50 Congolese worship in Kinshasa in the manner of unprogrammed Friends. Government authorities in Rwanda categorized Friends as a potentially dangerous cult because they did not use water baptism as a mark of membership.

Churches in the region continued to grow despite the ongoing violence. They acted together with Friends Peace Teams to develop a reconciliation center in Bujumbura, Burundi, and were active in monitoring the 2010 elections. Rwandan Friends engage in active peacebuilding, trauma healing, and reconciliation activity with people of all ages. Friends Peace House in Kigali is one center for this work. Rwandan Friends are actively combating HIV/AIDS, and in this and all other work gender equality is central.

LATIN AMERICA

After a gap of nearly two centuries (see Chapter 3), Quakerism returned to the Caribbean and Central America with mission work in Mexico (1871) and Jamaica (1881), and church planting by North American missionaries starting in Cuba in 1898 and

Guatemala in 1901. There are now substantial numbers of Quakers in Honduras, El Salvador, and especially Guatemala (with nearly 20,000 members), who have done much of their own outreach to establishing new churches. As in the rest of the world, each yearly meeting has its own sense of Quaker faith and practice but all are predominantly evangelical. Monteverde Monthly Meeting in Costa Rica is the main unprogrammed meeting in the region. Cuba Yearly Meeting has significant relationships with North American Friends from both Friends United Meeting and Friends General Conference.

The largest Latin America communities are in the high Andes of Bolivia, with 28,500 members in six yearly meetings. A key figure in Bolivian Quakerism was William Abel, who grew up among the Kumeyaay Tribe in California. He died soon after his arrival in Bolivia, but not before meeting and mentoring the young Bolivian Christian Juan Ayllon who experienced a call to ministry in 1919. Ayllon then attended the Friends' seminary in Guatemala. With his wife Tomasa Valle he returned to Bolivia in 1924 with help from the Friends Mission and the young national church in Central America. Together they set the groundwork for what was to become Iglesia Nacional Evangélica "Los Amigos" Boliviana which later came under the care of Oregon Yearly Meeting (now Northwest Yearly Meeting). Early priorities focused on evangelistic outreach, church planting, and local leadership development, along with adult literacy and education for children. An example of early evangelistic efforts comes from a report by Juan Ayllon where he described his encounter with some Aymara:

> In that place [we] found hungry souls. In the first meeting, after having heard the message, they sought the Lord at the altar. We told them that we were sent to those of their class, to the victims of sin, superstition and darkness, to the weary and heavy-laden ones, that they might find rest of the soul. We had meetings with them six Sundays, and not a meeting passed without an altar service ... In the six months that we have been here, we have been at the front of the battle, not only carrying the responsibility and burden in our hearts of preaching the Gospel. But also the weight of the bitter pain of so many perishing people falls upon us.
>
> (Quoted in Angell and Dandelion 2018, p. 185)

Missionaries to Central and South America came from yearly meetings in the United States including Indiana in 1919, California, and Oregon, all heavily influenced by the Holiness Movement of the mid-1880s. The Holiness Movement expected members to have a conversion experience, and complete sanctification (sometimes called the "Second Blessing"). In Latin America Scripture is given primary authority and correct doctrine is emphasized. Becoming a good Christian is more central than being identifiably Quaker. For instance, decisions are often based on consensus, but it is not unusual for groups to vote for the election of yearly meeting officers and other issues. Pastors are universal, but congregations are often poor and can pay little, so most hold other jobs.

Many Latin American friends tell stories of growing up in difficult circumstances, then encountering the Bible and/or a Friends Church that opened up a new life for them, changing not only their behavior but their attitude towards life. Guatemalan pastor Manuel de Jesus Coronado, for example, testified in a Friends church that Jesus gave him reason to live and also impelled him to share his story and gather others around him. As in Kenya, the Quaker reputation for honesty and sobriety meant that the government sought out Friends to fill jobs because they could be trusted.

Quaker missionaries of the early twentieth century faced not only the physical challenge of working at 12,500 foot altitude but the struggles to understand and work with people who had for centuries been oppressed by the upper classes in their own country and who spoke the difficult Aymara language. All missionaries spoke Spanish and some learned Aymara in the field. In addition, the Roman Catholics priests treated Protestants as seditious heretics. Allied with the aristocracy, Catholics had the power to persecute those they considered to be non-believers.

In Bolivia, along with a few small groupings, there are three large bodies of Friends. The largest yearly meeting is Iglesia Santidad de los Amigos (Holiness Friends). It has an estimated 20,000 members and operates 30 schools. It has no formal relations with Quaker groups outside Bolivia. Iglesia Nacional Evangélica "Los Amigos" Boliviana (INELA) has connections to Northwest Yearly Meeting, an Oregon yearly meeting with ties to EFCI.

Iglesia Evangélica Amigos Central (Central Friends) is an out-growth of the Holiness Movement in the United States with connections to Central Yearly Meeting in Indiana. Amigos Santidad and Amigos Central formed in the 1920s and 1930s and are affiliated with Friends World Committee for Consultation (see Chapter 6) and are centered in La Paz.

Another significant expansion of the Bolivian church was in Amacari villages on the shores of Lake Titicaca. Several accounts of this growth exist, but the ministry of local converts such as Cruz Chipana and Manuel Alvarado was fundamental to acceptance of the gospel message, and these faith communities eventually became part of the INELA Friends church in Bolivia. In the 1960s, Quakers spread from this area into Peru, forming Iglesia Nacional Evangélica "Los Amigos" del Peru.

The three large Bolivian yearly meetings have schools and officers or committees concerned with education, health, social welfare, and agricultural improvement and economic develop-ment. In the beginning teacher salaries were covered by mission funds but gradually came under local sponsorship. Soon trained nationals took over the teaching. At one point, according to Emma Condori, Friends had the largest Aymara church and were the third largest Bolivian denomination. There are many professionals among the Quakers in La Paz, some of whom established a Comité de Servicio Cuaquero en Bolivia, modeled on the British Friends Service Council. In the late 1990s, the NWYM mission established the Centro Teológico los Amigos (Friends Theological Center) for students at the Universidad Evangélica Boliviana (Evangelical University of Bolivia), and invited Diego Chuyma as its first director. It was open to Friends from all the different groupings. This century has seen interest in more cross-visitation for schools and individuals and a desire to create a Friends Center in Cochabamba where visitors can acclimate to the altitude as well as provide a venue for conferences and workshops.

By the 1950s pastoring, teaching, and administration were shifting from missionaries to the Aymara nationals, with national evangelists reaching out and planting new churches. In general, the missions supported and encouraged this development. Jack Willcuts notes that in the 1970s pastors were generally part time and might be an elder in the community or a teen-ager with spiritual gifts. Most pastors have been men, although this is slowly changing. INELA has a few women pastors. Manuela Calisaya de Alanguia, a Peruvian minister, describes her reluctance to take up leadership and personal shyness, but proclaims how God can use each person and prepare them for the ministry. Bible classes are mostly held separately for men and for women among some holiness churches, but INELA integrates men and women. Sunday services can run for three hours and are filled with prayers and song as well as a sermon. There are also small groups of Friends who meet from time to time in unprogrammed worship.

Quakers in Latin America differ from other Protestants in several ways. During the 1932 war between Bolivia and Paraguay, the government heavily recruited soldiers from among the Aymara, particularly from poorer families, which included many Friends. Some young men became conscientious objectors and carried guns to the front lines, but refused to use them. Others testified to their unwillingness to take another life, one stating: "I am a soldier of Jesus." The peace testimony is gradually becoming more widely accepted, especially among younger Friends (in Angell and Dandelion 2018, p. 189).

The structure of the Friends Church is minimally hierarchal with the local Church Council and the monthly meeting having the authority for final decision-making. The spiritual nature of the sacraments of baptism and communion is recognized but, in a context dominated by Catholicism and Aymara animism, converts may leave seeking a church where they can receive a public baptism. Friends have welcomed Spanish-language translations of Barclay and other early Quaker writing to help them articulate this understanding. Bernabé Sanchez, who for many years was a leader among Honduran Friends, reports experiences similar to George Fox, having his life transformed. He describes his faith this way: "Bible reading, going to worship services, prayer—that's all good but it's not complete if we don't know the author of the Bible." A summary of Latin American Quakerism in 2018 argued that common threads among Latin American Friends are "personal conversion, gathering of like-minded believers into local congregations, an emphasis on Jesus as the living word of God and on the Scriptures as the written words, and the preaching of a Christocentric gospel that encourages people to live like Jesus and to carry forth his ministry in the world around them" (in Angell and Dandelion 2018, pp. 187–8).

Since the 1970s, contacts with other Quaker groups such as Friends World Committee for Consultation have become increasingly important within the region and for connections with the Quaker community and practice worldwide. Bolivians may practice a subdued form of worship at conferences but their worship becomes livelier and more participatory once the outsiders leave. The cultural threads of music with native instruments and celebration are vibrant expressions of spirituality. From the start, missionaries have attempted to encourage the development of practices that flow naturally from indigenous traditions dating to the ancient cultures of the Incas and the Tiwanakotas. As reported in Angell and Dandelion (2018, p. 193):

> Because of this animistic background, many Latin American Quakers are aware of the power of evil and do not take lightly the seriousness of being cursed. They are also open to the many ways God can communicate to his people, including dreams and visions. They tend to be more open to the supernatural realm than are their fellow Quakers to the north.

Convinced Bolivian Quakers see Christianity as a gospel of hope and freedom from spiritual and physical imprisonment. The creation of schools, health care, and other actions towards social justice made the kingdom of God alive around them so they might feel "the sparkle of the Holy Spirit" in the words of Emma Condori Mamami (2017, p 6, 7).

ASIA AND THE WEST PACIFIC: CROSSING CULTURES

The three largest yearly meetings in Asia and the west Pacific region are the evangelical bodies in Nepal, India, Bhutan, Taiwan, and Indonesia, followed by the liberal unprogrammed meetings in Australia and Aotearoa/New Zealand. The number of Friends in the region has almost doubled since 2007, reaching 24,000 in 2017.

Quakerism arrived in Aotearoa/New Zealand and Australia early in the nineteenth century. James Backhouse, responding to an inward call, visited Australia beginning in 1832, He documented the condition of settlers, of convicts who had been deported from England, and of Aboriginal peoples, and he started Australia's first meeting in Hobart, in the unprogrammed tradition. The Friends boarding school in Hobart was founded in 1887, and continues with many Asian students as well as local Friends. The first meeting for worship in Aotearoa/New Zealand dates to 1842 and a school was active in the mid-twentieth century. Unprogrammed meetings are found in all the major cities and Friends in both nations hold a strong concern for the peace testimony, care for the environment, and bicultural relations.

The Foreign Missions Association of London Yearly Meeting sent missionaries to China, Madagascar, India, and Sri Lanka beginning in 1884. Americans from Ohio, mainly women, soon joined them. Both groups made schools and hospitals a higher priority than building churches. By the 1930s there were over 300 members in Nanjing. During World War II North American Friends operated in China caring for the wounded and providing relief work. After 1949, the establishment of the People's Republic of China severely limited Christian activity. American Friends from Ohio arrived in Taiwan in 1953 with a focus on evangelism and church planting. The missionaries encouraged local leadership so that there were 36 self-supporting congregations with over 3,000 members by 2010 and Taiwanese Friends were sending missionaries to the Philippines and Hong Kong, where there are also small unprogrammed meetings for worship.

Japan and Korea both have unprogrammed worship and sustain a strong focus on the peace testimony. The Korean pacifist, Ham Sok Han and the prominent Japanese figure Inazo Nitobe were members of Quaker meetings. Reconciliation between the North and South has been an important goal for Korean Friends who have worked with the American Friends Service Committee and the Alternatives to Violence Project. The Friends Girls' School established in Tokyo in 1887 remains active with about 800 students, and Japanese Friends have also been leaders in support for senior citizens.

Friends in India and Nepal represent the variety of Quaker practice. In Calcutta, Indians were led to start a meeting for worship after reading Quaker literature. Elsewhere, Friends influenced by Rabindranath Tagore or Mohandas Gandhi moved to India to be part of interfaith work and the practice of non-violence, or simply to study Hindi. American Friends Douglas and Dorothy Steere worked to build relations among Hindus, Buddhists, and Christians in India and Japan. More traditional mission work took hold, particularly in Bundelkhand by evangelical Friends who opened a school for Hindu girls. The General Conference of Friends in India formed in 1959 to bring together Friends across the nation annually and to help support the scattered meetings that have sometimes faced hostility because of the association of Christianity with British rule. In 1994, Indian friends began mission work in Nepal where there are over 1,000 worshipers by 2010 and many who have participated in the Alternatives to Violence Project.

EUROPE AND THE MIDDLE EAST: UNITY AND STABILITY

Britain Yearly Meeting is by far the largest in Europe with 20,000 members and active attenders. In total, the number of Friends in the region has grown from 23,000 in 2007 to over 32,000 in 2017, largely by the establishment of evangelical churches in countries such as Hungary with 4000 and Romania with 1000. Ireland Yearly Meeting, with 2000 members, includes both Eire and Northern Ireland. Western European yearly meetings represent entire countries, have fewer than 500 members each, and worship out of the expectant silence without a pastor.

From the earliest days, traveling Friends took the message of George Fox beyond the British Isles. They initiated what turned out to be an irregular and interrupted Quaker presence on the Continent and in the Mediterranean, in contrast to the continuity of Quakerism in the United States and Canada. Small groups of Friends gathered in Amsterdam and in Germany in the late seventeenth century but they were not long-lived. Small groups also formed in France (1785), Norway (1818), and Denmark (1875). However, a strong Quaker presence on the Continent is more recent, linked to service work in the aftermath of twentieth-century wars. Several Western European nations now have yearly meetings, largely in the unprogrammed, liberal tradition. The Quaker Council for European Affairs was established in Brussels in 1979 to bring Quaker concerns before European decision-makers.

After decades of outreach to peace groups in the Soviet Union and running conferences for diplomats from both sides of the Iron Curtain to meet, a small group began to meet in Moscow in the late 1980s "after the manner of Friends," at the home of historian Tatiana Pavlova and now at Friends House Moscow. The twenty-first century has also seen the growth of evangelical church planting particularly among Roma peoples of Eastern Europe.

First-generation Quakers also ventured beyond Europe to Jerusalem and Constantinople, but the first meeting in western Asia was at Brummana, Lebanon in 1868. Another formed soon after in Ramallah, near Jerusalem. The associated Quaker schools have gained a reputation for educational excellence. Ramallah Friends School offers the only International Baccalaureate program in Palestine and seeks to affirm testimonies such as peace and equality to a student body of both Christians and Muslims.

The active center of European Quakerism remains Britain and Ireland. British Friends avoided the separations that tore apart American yearly meetings. Contemporary British Quakerism has its roots in changes in the second part of the nineteenth century. In the 1850s and 1860s, rules on disownment were relaxed and other reforms led to an increase in membership, while Friends gained full civil rights in 1870. British Friends generally welcomed new biblical scholarship that put the Bible in historical context. Theological diversity increased throughout the twentieth century and growing numbers of British Friends do not consider them-selves Christian. In 1993, a small conservative yearly meeting was formed as a Christian body who worshipped out of the expectant silence. The much larger Britain Yearly Meeting has held to unprogrammed worship of their spiritual ancestors and sought to create a space where the newer, more universalist spirituality can be held in creative tension with the early Quaker theology. The yearly meeting has sought to reverse declines in membership by active outreach to the general public, helped by its longstanding engagement in support of peace and justice issues.

Friends have been active in Ireland since 1654, and they con-tinue to hold unprogrammed worship centuries later. Irish Friends embrace a wide theological range within a single yearly meeting, although tending somewhat more centrist Christian than continental meetings.

TWENTIETH-CENTURY NORTH AMERICA: REUNIFICATION AND NEW SEPARATIONS

North America has roughly 85,000 Quakers spread geographically from Florida north to Canadian Yearly Meeting, and west to the liberal, unprogrammed Alaska Friends Conference and to evangelical Alaska Yearly Meeting. The largest North American bodies are the Evangelical Friends Church Eastern Region, based in Ohio, the liberal, unprogrammed Philadelphia Yearly Meeting, and the Evangelical Friends Church Southwest in California. Overall North American membership has dropped by approximately 6,000 since 2007.

The upheavals and wars that scarred the twentieth century caused many Friends to focus their energies on witnessing to the need for peace and justice in the world (see Chapter 6). It was also a period of change for the Religious Society of Friends. Holiness theology, evangelicalism, and a concern for right doctrine continued to flavor meetings and churches in the United States as they hired pastors and welcomed a more structured form of worship. In the same decades, more liberal meetings that continued to worship out of the silence embraced aspects of modern critical theology, universalism, and the social gospel. These meetings, which are often politically as well as theologically liberal, are centered in the eastern states and in urban centers and university towns across the country. Canada is similar with roughly half of Canadian Quakers in Ontario and other unprogrammed meetings found coast to coast.

There were consequences for the organization of the Religious Society of Friends. Branches that had angrily separated in the nineteenth century found it harder and harder to care about old arguments. Pressured by younger Friends, they began a decades-long process of reunification (see Chapter 3). At the same time, beginning in the 1920s, some of the churches most attracted to the Holiness Movement separated themselves from the newly formed body of Friends now known as Friends United Meeting (FUM), eventually coming together as Evangelical Friends Church International (EFCI).

North American Quakerism in the twenty-first century has been marked by conflicting patterns of separations and consolidations revolving around questions of authority. Some Friends have increasingly placed more authority in the hands of church leadership as a way to promote a uniform theology and practice. Others are open to allowing individual discretion in matters of belief and restructured their meetings to limit hierarchy. Oscar Lugusa Malande, a Kenyan Friend, has described this non-hierarchical understanding:

> The authority existing within the hierarchy of leadership in the church, if not well exercised, can create deficiency and imbalance in the running of church affairs. In Quakerism, the expectation is that everyone equally participates in doing ministry. As people gather in the presence of God for service in worship, all barriers of inequality have to be brought down.
>
> (2019, p. 32)

The traditional Quaker expectation that the whole congregation has responsibility for ministry is at odds with many Protestant or evangelical bodies who give substantial authority to the pastor and a defined lay leadership. Because many pastors in Quaker churches come from other denominations, it is sometimes hard for Quakers to practice their ideal. Quaker scholar Cherice Bock describes the contrasting pulls of Quakerism and evangelicalism, which she sees embodied in the history of Oregon Yearly Meeting (now Northwest Yearly Meeting):

> With a peace testimony that differed from most other evangelicals and an understanding of Christianity differing from other Friends, Oregon Yearly Meeting [OYM] expressed what Timothy Burdick calls "American neo-evangelical Quakerism," sometimes leaning toward fundamentalism and sometimes expressing a social gospel interpretation of Friends ... The fluctuations in OYM's willingness to work with the AFSC exemplify this dilemma.
>
> (2019, pp. 22, 23)

These competing tendencies are a clear example of the tensions between cultural influences, an individual's inner discernment, and the difficulties of living with integrity while working with those who see the world and read the Bible differently. Even as Northwest Yearly Meeting upheld the peace testimony as integral to the teachings of Jesus, they also emphasized authority and biblical literalism and were skeptical of liberal social justice work in the early part of the century. Towards the 1940s the social gospel became more acceptable, yet Oregon Quakers continued to be among those cautious about interacting with non-Christians. In the twenty-first century Northwest Yearly Meeting split and a new body, Sierra-Cascades Yearly Meeting (SCYM), formed as a body which is Christian but open and affirming of all people and passionate about social justice action in many forms (see Chapter 7).

In New England, and elsewhere on the East Coast, modernism took hold in the early twentieth century. Peace and social justice work became primary for many Friends and freedom of thought and action flourished in the environment of unprogrammed worship. Rufus Jones, a teacher at Haverford College and a prolific writer about Quakerism and mystical Christianity, entranced many with his down-home Maine sense of humor. He is the most widely known of the ministers and scholars who embraced modernist biblical scholarship and articulated mysticism as central to early Friends and modern worship. Studies at Harvard with philosophers Josiah Royce and William James influenced his focus on the individual religious experience and his belief that the traditional institutional structures of Quakerism were useful but not essential. He helped to re-center Quaker worship on the direct experience of the divine, whether reached through Christian understandings or through other spiritual traditions. He taught Quakerism as ecumenical, tolerant, and congregational. The understanding that Quaker worship is a process of directly opening oneself to the divine recaptures the experience of early Friends like Isaac Penington and Robert Barclay. It has been the most fruitful way in which modern unprogrammed Friends have explored their faith and worship. It has given birth to powerful devotional writing, particularly Thomas Kelly's *A Testament of Devotion* (1941). "That of God in everyone," a phrase that Jones popularized as a restatement of the concept of the Inward Light, has become the guiding concept for liberal Friends as a basis of faith and an affirmation of human commonality.

In the early twenty-first century it is not only acceptable for liberal Quakers to reject Christianity, perhaps seeing themselves as

Jewish and Quaker or Buddhist and Quaker, or occasionally to view themselves as non-theist. In contrast to evangelical Friends churches, which stress biblical authority as understood by the leadership, liberal meetings find that the pressure toward individualism can mean that some members reject any authority from the community. There is also discomfort and tension in some unprogrammed meetings between those who see their faith as mystical and others who come to be among other political activists. The latter at times grow frustrated when the entire meeting does not support their particular cause. Support for sexual minorities and gay marriage became a defining issue beginning in the 1970s. Many liberal meetings struggled before finding unity to honor same-sex marriages. When evangelical bodies addressed the same issue, the frequent result has been disagreement about morality, biblical interpretations, and the source of authority, with divisions and separations as a result (see Chapter 7).

MINISTERS, MISSIONARIES, OR ACADEMICS

Three and a half centuries after its origins as a profoundly prophetic movement that stressed the unity of the Spirit and the potential for every individual to hear the voice of Christ within, Friends have found that even within their small numbers they encompass much of the range of North American Christianity. The issues they face in regard to the biblical interpretation, authority versus individualism, social inclusiveness, and ecumenism are also dividing lines in many other denominations.

This chapter has generalized approaches and beliefs, but the reality is always more complex at the scale of individual churches and meetings. Our own monthly meeting is solidly liberal in most meanings of that word, yet has active members who are passionately Christian and members who consider themselves refugees from Christianity. Others might quote Sufi poetry, recount personal struggles, or report on political demonstrations. One of our challenges as a community is how to "listen in tongues" so that every person can use the spiritual language that resonates in their soul and be treated with respect.

One way to consider changes over the generations among Friends is in the words we use to describe the roles of public

Friends. For most of Quaker history, such individuals were known as ministers. They were expected to articulate the common faith through offering spontaneous messages in worship as led by the Light of Christ. For the past century, Friends have looked to and written about missionaries who courageously travel to foreign countries to share their faith, and also to scholars who articulate the history, practice, and theology of Friends. Friends have written about their faith from the early days of pamphleteering, to the wide practice of spiritual journals, to the modern proliferation of devotional and academic books. Missionaries often tell stories of faith with the hope of bringing more people into belief. Academics have an ethic of objectivity and would likely cite the Quaker emphasis on truth-telling as central to their purpose. The writing of journals, essentially the spiritual autobiographies of ministers, continues, although the practice is somewhat buried in the sheer volume of academic work.

Quaker literature is gradually being translated into Spanish as agreement has developed on the appropriate vocabulary for unique Quaker terms. Voices from the Global South are finding their way into print with British and North American publishers. Friends World Committee for Consultation (see Chapter 7) is working to reverse the long-standing practice of one-way visitation by individuals from wealthier nations traveling among African and Latin American Friends. It will take many years to see how this will change the Religious Society of Friends in numbers, theology, styles of worship, and business practice.

NOTES

1 Missionary work in Africa, Latin America, and Asia was originally carried out by British Friends and by American Friends from the Midwest, associated with Friends United Meeting, or from the US West Coast, associated with Evangelical Friends Church International. British and Midwestern Friends shared a similar biblical orientation in the nineteenth century. In many ways, FUM remained a middle ground for Quakerism in the twentieth century. On one side, Britain and the US, East Coast meetings shifted in a theologically liberal direction in the twentieth century. On the other, Oregon Yearly Meeting split off from Five Years Meeting (the future FUM) in 1926 to follow more vigorously evangelical leadings, joining Ohio, Kansas, and Rocky Mountain yearly meetings in forming Evangelical Friends Alliances in 1965. They were joined by California

(Southwest) and Alaska yearly meetings to form what is now Evangelical Friends Church International-North America in 1994.

2 Official membership figures tend to undercount the number of individuals who participate regularly in meetings and churches without formally joining.

FURTHER READING

Margery Post Abbott and Peggy Senger Parsons, *Walk Worthy of Your Calling: Quakers and the Traveling Ministry* (Richmond, IN: Friends United Press, 2004). Reflections from Friends of all backgrounds.

Zablon Isaac Malenge, *Quakerism in the Perspective of the Friends Church in Kenya* (Kenya: Diana Books Library Services, 2003).

Ron Stansell, *Missions by the Spirit: Learning from Quaker Examples* (Newberg, OR: Barclay Press, 2009). An evangelical Quaker missionary describes the transition from missionary outreach to the growth of independent Quaker churches in Bolivia.

David Zarembka, *A Peace of Africa: Reflections on Life in the Great Lakes Region* (Washington, DC: Madera Press, 2011).

A SECRET POWER AMONG THEM
WORSHIP AND PRACTICE

When you come to your meetings ... do you sit down in True Silence, resting from your own Will and Workings, and waiting upon the Lord, with your minds fixed in that Light wherewith Christ has enlightened you, until the Lord breathes life in you, and prepares you, and your spirits and souls, to make you fit for his service, that you may offer unto him, a pure and spiritual sacrifice?

(William Penn, "A Tender Visitation," *The Select Works of William Penn*, 1771, p. 441)

Members of the Society of Friends in the twenty-first century worship in multiple ways, but their shared goal is to be open to the divine spirit in the way that William Penn prescribed more than three centuries ago. Many evangelical Quaker churches in the United States, Africa, and Latin America employ paid pastors, and conduct worship services similar to those in a Methodist or Nazarene church. Other meetings, primarily in Britain, Europe, New Zealand, Australia, and North America but found on every continent, continue the tradition of expectant, silent waiting. They worship listening for the Spirit and knowing that any participant might rise and offer vocal ministry to the gathered community. Friends have also adopted distinctive language and practices for many of the concerns and activities that are part of the life of a religious congregation, and this chapter tries to demystify some of the terminology peculiar to Friends.

This chapter is a field guide to contemporary Quaker practice around the world. A distinctive type of unprogrammed worship and community decision-making was common to all Friends for almost two centuries. It continues in Europe and North America even as divisions of the nineteenth century and global spread in the twentieth century have led to important and vital variations on the original. The chapter tacks back and forth among the different contemporary practices. It begins with evolving styles of Quaker worship around the world and then describes the ways in which Quakers organize themselves into worshiping congregations and larger groupings. The following section explores the importance of community and group discernment as a balance to the inherent individualism of Quaker theology. The final section examines the distinctive way in which Quakers make decisions.

One way to understand differences and commonalities among different flavors of Friends is with a diagram developed by Conservative Friend Bill Taber (Figure 5.1). It shows pairs of opposites across the circle (for example, individual versus corporate inspiration) but also highlights a common center. Early Friends were able to hold these extremes in creative tension. Later Friends have tended to move toward the edges of the circle. Different groupings such as British Friends and Irish Friends, several Bolivian yearly meetings, or the various national groups in the United States understand their placement in distinctive ways. In short, there is no simple continuum from liberal to pastoral to evangelical, but rather a continual interplay across many dimensions. Although we sometimes use "liberal, unprogrammed," "programmed," and "evangelical" as shorthand for predominant types of Friends, many churches and meetings flourish between the extremes (see "convergent Friends" in Chapter 7).

Underpinning all of these practices is a belief in the transcendent experience available in group worship. The short phrase in the chapter title is taken from a larger passage in which early Quaker theologian Robert Barclay described his first experience of Quaker worship:

> [W]hen I came into the silent assemblies of God's people, I felt a secret power among them, which touched my heart; and as I gave way unto it I found the evil weakening in me and the good raised up; and so I became thus knit and united unto them, hungering more and more after the increase of this power and life whereby I might feel myself perfectly redeemed.

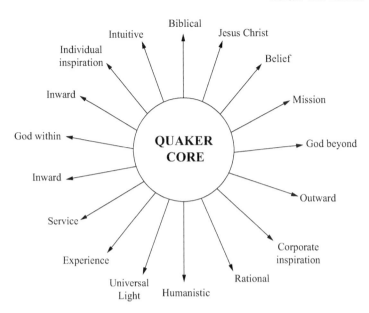

Figure 5.1 Paradoxical Quaker extremes
Based on William Taber, *Fostering Vital Friends Meetings Part Two* (Friends General Conference)

By "secret" he did not mean something deliberately hidden, but rather a mystical experience available to all people that was profoundly different from the standardized worship in the Church of England and that he found only within Quaker worship.

STYLES OF WORSHIP

A century ago, when Carl's mother was growing up in a small Ohio town, she would play a game with her cousin that they called "Quaker Meeting." Two little girls sat as still as they could, stared at each other, maybe begin to fidget or make faces, and eventually broke into uncontrollable giggles. There were substantial numbers of Quakers in western Ohio and eastern Indiana, although none in her town. Its churches in those years were Lutheran, Methodist, and Evangelical United Brethren. Local residents likely knew three things about Quakers: they talked oddly with "thee" and "thou," they wore old-fashioned clothes (the oatmeal box image was already in wide circulation), and they met in sober silence.

"Silent meeting" and "silent worship" are misnomers, even though commonly used by insiders and outsiders. Silence for its own sake is not the goal. A common description for many Quaker meetings that continue the early style of worship is "unprogrammed," meaning that there is no predetermined sequence of actions, and that what happens emerges spontaneously. Quakers sit in *expectant silent waiting* or *stillness*, trying to turn away from the own thoughts (easier said than done when there is a busy week ahead) and hoping to open themselves to the experience of the divine. Early Friends were clear that a meeting began in silence "watching in holy dependence on the Lord and meeting not only outwardly in one place, but inwardly in the one Spirit," in the words of Robert Barclay. When words were spoken or prayers offered, they were understood to be inspired by God's spirit. This is not God capturing one's tongue and turning you into an oracle, but your own words as shaped and motivated by divine presence. When Friends sometimes talk about gathered meetings, they are not referring to the physical get-together but to the sense that the divine spirit is present and accessible to everyone in the room—in the words of Thomas Kelly in *The Gathered Meeting*, "the sense is present that a new Life and Power has entered into our midst."

Friends over the centuries have tried to put their experience of worship into words, a serious challenge when it is intensely individual and communal at the same time, and often a mystical experience that goes beyond words. In the language of 1658, here is how George Fox instructed a fellow seeker:

> Be still and cool in thy own mind and spirit from thy own thoughts, and then thou wilt feel the principle of God to turn thy mind to the Lord God, whereby thou wilt receive his strength and power from whence life comes, to allay all tempests, against blusterings and storms. That is it which moulds up into patience, into innocency, into soberness, into stillness, into quietness, up to God, with his powers.

Fox's contemporary Isaac Penington, one of the most important and eloquent among early Quakers, emphasized the importance of settling into worship by stilling everyday concerns to be open to

God. In modern terms, he knew that it was easy to come to meeting for worship and start using the quiet to plan the coming week or go over old worries rather than listening for the still, small voice of the Spirit. It is fine to come to worship having prepared with meditation or reading, but unprogrammed Friends are usually wary about bringing a fully formed message. Feeling the impulse to speak, they might ask the following questions: Are these simply my own thoughts that are best saved for conversation outside of worship? If they come from outside myself, is the message meant for me alone? If it is a message meant for the group, is *now* the time when it must be shared? When certain about all of these questions, then rise to speak.[1]

BOX 5.1 ISAAC PENINGTON, "SOME DIRECTIONS TO THE PANTING SOUL," 1661

The following passage from Penington's many writings is one of the most frequently cited descriptions of the essence of Quaker worship, as relevant in the present century as in the 1600s:

> So then, there is the sweet communion ... the sweet joy and refreshment in the Lord our righteousness, who causeth righteousness to drop down from heaven, and truth to spring up out of the earth. And so our Father is felt blessing us, blessing our land, blessing our habitations, delighting in us and over us to do us good; and our land yields its increase to the Lord of Life, who hath redeemed it and planted the precious plants and seeds of life in it ...

> Give over thine own willing, give over thy own running, give over thine own desiring to know or be anything and sink down to the seed which God sows in the heart, and let that grow in thee and be in thee and breathe in thee and act in thee; and thou shalt find by sweet experience that the Lord knows that and loves and owns that, and will lead it to the inheritance of Life, which is its portion.

Individuals with an experience of Buddhism can be attracted to unprogrammed meetings because of the similarity of group contemplation. Some maintain parallel Buddhist and Quaker practices. The intent of meeting for worship, however, is quite different from individual meditation, for it is a community or corporate activity in which silent waiting is itself a ministry to the group. The purpose of that waiting is not to empty one's mind, but to open it to a larger presence that may lead to a sense of wholeness with the group and sometimes to spoken ministry.

If Isaac Penington or Robert Barclay were to visit a twenty-first-century meeting for worship in Britain or Australia, he would likely find it anemic. Early Friends met for hours at a time rather than for a carefully monitored 60 minutes, just as likely standing in a barn as sitting on a ring of comfortable chairs. In a culture based on oratory and public speaking, early Friends would often offer extended sermons, especially to seekers, that might last for hours. Members of the current time-obsessed culture, modern Quakers in the Euro-American tradition speak for minutes rather than hours at a time. Their messages range from Bible references to Sufi poetry; they include comments on the problems of the world and stories of personal pain and struggles as well as more clearly "religious" or spiritual messages. An hour may pass with no spoken messages, or a handful, or a large number; when ministries follow in quick succession, Quakers may comment on the "popcorn meeting" in which one person after another pops up to speak (the spiritual popcorn can sometimes be quite nourishing).

Unprogrammed meetings seek to strike a careful theological balance between their Christian heritage and their attractiveness for a large number of unchurched seekers. Meetings are likely to include members and attenders who are convinced Christians, but also those who are refugees from strict Christian upbringing. Experience with rigid rules and hellfire-and-damnation preaching makes them sensitive or even hostile to messages that draw on the Bible or even the most liberal Christian theology. Some participants may reject references to God. Others may have been drawn to Quakers for their peace testimony and social activism and may even find meeting for worship a distraction from what they think should be the real business of the meeting. A successful meeting establishes a climate in which a wide spectrum of beliefs and messages are accepted in the spirit of love and truth in which they are offered. In sum, contemporary unprogrammed meetings preserve the belief of early Friends in the capacity of anyone to deliver a message of spiritual depth and power, but they differ in specifics of outward form (or at least in physical comfort) and in content.

Members of Friends churches in many parts of the United States, in Latin America, and in East Africa have a quite different Sunday morning experience. Worship at a Friends church in the US can surprise anyone expecting to gather in silence. Most North American Friends churches have pastors who often prepare a printed order of service along with names of those who take on various roles that Sunday morning—hence "programmed" as differentiated from "unprogrammed" or "open" worship. The variations in American programmed meetings range from lightly organized worship where someone may give a short message and offer a Bible reading or hymn to services where a period of open worship is an invitation for messages, songs, and prayer requests. Christian rock-music bands, extensive preaching and prayer, and formal altar calls may be part of worship at a Friends church. Pastors usually have a prepared sermon, but they sometimes arrive on Sunday morning and realize their words are not what the congregation is hungering for, set the text aside, and call instead for open worship or deliver a different message.

Attendance at a Friends church in Guatemala or Kenya can be an exuberant experience and a bit of a shock to introverted (dare we say stodgy) Americans and Europeans anticipating a more contemplative experience. Evangelical Quaker missionaries in Africa often brought with them a style of church service that follows an order of worship common to non-liturgical Protestant denominations like Methodists and Baptists. These practices of hymn singing, prayers, and message from a paid pastor or lay minister may be blended with local traditional styles of music, prayer, or dancing.

Although there are important exceptions in the United States and Africa, pastors worldwide often come from other evangelical denominations with little understanding or appreciation of Quaker heritage. There are a limited number of seminaries and pastoral training programs associated with Quaker universities or with an explicit Quaker focus. The result is to move some Friends churches further into the evangelical mainstream. In Africa and also in Mexico, the clerk may take a key role in organizing worship rather than a pastor.

Prayer is central in most Quaker communities during times of communal worship, in the home, and at other gatherings. The pastor may be called on as a mediator to God in contrast to the traditional Quaker assertion that no mediator is needed as all people have the capacity to hear God's voice. In Africa the phrase "the blood of Jesus" is a call for protection that builds on the pre-Christian tradition of blood sacrifice to appease evil spirits. African Friends may also hold *keshas* or overnight prayer events for spiritual and emotional renewal popular with the youth. Unprogrammed Friends are unusual in their discomfort with vocal prayer, pre-ferring to go into the silence as they hold a person or a situation "in the Light" of divine love.

Friends in Latin America and elsewhere experience pressure from Catholics or other Christians about the absence of the out-ward sacraments. Friends World Committee for Consultation works to translate key Quaker texts into Spanish. So does New England Yearly Meeting, which maintains a sister relationship with Cuba Yearly Meeting. These have helped Latin American Friends articulate the theological basis of baptism and communion as inward experiences that do not depend on the outward use of water, wine, and wafers. However, on most every continent there are some Friends who value these outward sacraments and incorporate them into their worship.

Much smaller numbers of Conservative Friends, found largely in North Carolina, Ohio, and Iowa, offer a different mix that com-bines unprogrammed worship with a strong Christian orientation. They see themselves as *conserving* the traditional Quakerism of the early generations in the face of variations in theology among the more numerous liberal unprogrammed meetings (which try to preserve older forms of worship but often tend toward universalist theology in place of explicit Christianity) and variations in practice among Friends churches (where traditional Quaker Christianity is modified by the use of paid ministers and more expressive worship). They retain a commitment to core Quaker testimonies with a strong orientation to divine guidance.

BOX 5.2   NINE CORE QUAKER BELIEFS

As articulated by Arthur Larrabee for the Quaker Speak website in 2018, these nine points resonate with many Friends from unprogrammed meetings, but are too open-ended for many other Friends.

1   **There is a living, dynamic, spiritual presence at work in the world which is both within us and outside of us.** Quakers use many names to describe this spiritual presence. Among the names we use are God, spirit, the light, the inward light, the inner light, Christ, truth, love.

2   **There is that of God in everyone.** This statement of belief is similar to the first statement, and Quakers will talk about there being that of God in everyone, and it is the belief that the creator has endowed each person with a measure of the divine essence, and that as a consequence, all of life is sacred and interconnected.

3   **Each person is capable of the direct and unmediated experience of God.** Our belief leads us into a form of worship that does not rely on clergy or liturgy or creed. Rather, we come together in the silence. We sometimes refer to our worship as "waiting worship." Waiting to hear—listen for—the still, small voice within, and listening for that of God—the still, small voice—speaking to us.

4   **Our understanding and experience of God is nurtured and enlarged in community.** When we come together in community, each of us brings our own manifestation of the divine energy. When we come together in community, we experience and embrace our diversity; we experience a much larger understanding and vision of God.

5   **The Bible is an important spiritual resource, and the life and teachings of Jesus are relevant for us today.** For many of us, the Bible is an inspired record of humankind's interaction with God through the ages. Quakers find that the truth and the teachings found in the Bible are an inspiration for daily living and also an inspiration for our worship together.

6   **The revelation of God's truth is continuing and ongoing.** Quakers are very clear that the revelation of God's truth did not end with the writing of the Bible. We believe that God has continued to reveal God's truth and make God's will and energy, truth—known to humankind down through the ages, down to the present day.

7   **We welcome truth from whatever source it may come.** We find that our experience of worship and our experience of the Divine is enriched by welcoming truth from different sources. We welcome spiritual truth from different sources.

8   **Our inward experience of God transforms us and leads us into outward expressions of faithful living, witness, and action.** Individually and collectively, we witness to God's presence in our lives by the way we live our lives and the way we model God's truth in the world. One of the consequences of listening for the inward voice and being led into outward expressions of faithful living and witness and action are Quaker testimonies. Testimonies that are well known today are testimonies of simplicity and peace and integrity, community, equality, and stewardship.

9   **Modeling God's presence in our lives is more important than espousing beliefs.** Quakers believe that the way we live our lives in of much more importance than what we say. There's an old Quaker expression, "Let your life speak," and that's very much a part of Quakerism: the understanding that the way we model God's truth in our lives is to let our lives speak it.

CONGREGATIONAL GOVERNANCE

The Society of Friends has historically emphasized the primacy of the local worshiping community, as the source of religious experience and as the decision-making body controlling its own membership and affairs. On the spectrum of church governance, Friends thus fall in the congregational side with Baptists and Disciples of Christ rather than with hierarchical churches such as Lutherans and Anglicans. The key building block is the community of Quakers who convene once a month to transact organizational business—adopt budgets, accept memberships and marriages, agree to service projects, approve political statements.

This said, a thicket of terminology can confuse newcomers and outsiders. In Kenya the core group is the village meeting, which holds membership, hires pastors, keeps records, and meets for worship every Sunday. In the United States this building-block community may be a Friends church, in the more Americanized branches, or a monthly meeting, on the unprogrammed side. The latter terminology can confuse outsiders, since "monthly" refers to the timing of meeting for business and not to the weekly meeting for worship. Many such groups now present themselves to the public as a Friends meeting, even if their official name may retain "monthly meeting." A monthly meeting may be an umbrella for one or more "worship groups," smaller clusters of Quakers, and seekers who meet separately and perhaps at a distance from the main meeting. "Preparative meetings" are newly formed groups that are being mentored toward independence. Normally monthly meetings hold property, although, as in Bolivia, some evangelical church property is held by the yearly meeting. As with other denominations, a large city may have several monthly/Friends meetings serving different parts of the city and each developing its own distinct character.

Quakers use different structures in different parts of the world. If one attends Sunday worship on the south side of Birmingham, England at Bourneville Quaker Meeting or Cotteridge Quaker Meeting, the experience seems very like that of an unprogrammed monthly meeting in the United States, with sometimes imposing meetinghouses, announcements after worship, and business meetings about "local Quaker matters." However, many of the important decisions are made at area meetings that embrace multiple "local meetings" (Central England Area Meeting includes Bournville, Cotteridge, and a dozen others). Area meetings in Britain are "the primary business meeting for Quakers" and approve marriages, hold membership, and have legal responsibility for property and employment.

Australians and New Zealanders use variations on the British model. Australians deal with their wide open spaces with a regional meeting for each of their states and the federal territory. Regional meetings own property, hold membership, and embrace local meetings and worshipping groups. In Aotearoa/New Zealand monthly meetings may include a variety of constituent groups that range from small worship groups to city meetings. They gather for major decisions in the larger city like Dunedin or Christchurch or central meetinghouses in Auckland or Wellington. East African Friends distinguish meetings by function, described in the 2002

Faith and Practice of Friends Church Kanisa la Marafiki as (1) worship to introduce people to salvation through Christ (2) worship for believers and visitors, and (3) meetings for business which are to be held in a spirit of prayer and worship, but at a separate time from weekly times of worship.

Overarching the different locally based meetings and worshipping groups are yearly meetings. As Australians put it, "the term *Yearly Meeting* is used by Quakers around the world to refer to a regional group of individual congregations which come together on an annual basis for business and spiritual purposes." Britain, Cuba, Canada, El Salvador, Ireland, Norway, Rwanda, Japan, Nepal, Honduras, and Jamaica have single yearly meetings. Mexico, Kenya, Burundi, Bolivia, and the United States have multiple yearly meetings distinguished by regional coverage and by theological or cultural bent. Yearly meetings interact by sending representatives to the national and international Quaker groups such as Friends World Committee for Consultation, United Society for Friends Women International, the American Friends Service Committee, Friends Church in Kenya, and Evangelical Friends Church International. Since the very early years when written letters were the only form of communication, yearly meetings at their annual gatherings also craft letters or epistles that summarize their own interests, concerns, and activities. They share those with other yearly meetings worldwide. The exchange of these epistles, often addressed "to Friends everywhere," ideally serves as a way for each of these independent groups to acknowledge their relationship.

Most yearly meetings publish a book of *Faith and Practice*, and revise it roughly once a generation. They are sometimes subtitled "a book of Christian discipline," where "discipline" refers to the standards and expectations of action. As the title implies, they offer both practical and spiritual guidance. On the practical side they may define the process for yearly meeting decisions, summarize the duties of yearly meeting committees, describe typical committees for the local meeting or church, and outline procedures for dealing with membership, marriages, and memorial services. The pastoral functions of care and counsel for members and attenders fall to committees in unprogrammed meetings and jointly to committees and paid staff in Friends churches.

Most books of *Faith and Practice* include a set of *queries*. Quakers have long used "queries" or "advices and queries" to establish common understanding of their faith and its expression. Queries originated as a practical expedient in seventeenth-century England where Friends were separated by distance and poor communication. Local groups shared written answers to common questions: What was the current membership? Was anyone in jail for their faith, and were they and their families cared for? Did the meeting have a strong spiritual base? In some yearly meetings, responses to these sorts of questions are addressed in annual "state of society" reports that may be shared at its annual gathering.

Modern queries are designed to be open-ended in order to encourage deeper reflection on the spiritual life of individuals and the community. They are a way for individuals and meetings to hold themselves accountable to standards of belief and behavior. In a sense they serve as an alternative to a formal creed. They are sometimes preceded by "advices," or statements of values and principles that Friends seek to follow individually and as communities. Queries ask about one's active relationship to the church or meeting, one's personal faith, and one's manner of living and concerns for society. The queries from a theologically liberal yearly meeting and an evangelical yearly meeting will be quite similar in topics and sometimes wording (although the latter will more often include "Christ," "Christian," and "God"): Do you live a life of simplicity and care for the Earth? Do you speak out for justice and morality? Do you have a personal devotional practice?

Faith and Practice volumes often provide guidance in one of two forms. Evangelical yearly meetings will usually offer explicit articles of faith including the text of George Fox's letter to the Governor of Barbados (1671), which was a careful justification of Quakers as fully Christian, and the Richmond Declaration (1887), which explained how American Quakers practiced Christianity. Unprogrammed Friends in contrast accompany the queries with quotations from spiritual writings from all five centuries in which Friends have been active. These excerpts, in the dozens and sometimes in the hundreds, offer openings for reflection and meditation. Quakers have always liked to write about their spiritual journeys and are equally fond of scouring those writings for phrases and paragraphs that "speak to their condition" to use a favorite Quaker phrase.

These responses come from classic Quaker writing by people like Margaret Fell and Isaac Penington, from more obscure letter writers and diarists, and from modern Friends who address the same issues of faith and spiritual experience in contemporary language.

A final point about Friends governance involves yearly meeting structure. Some yearly meetings are loose federations of local meetings that offer fellowship, resources, and the opportunity to take joint positions on important issues through the adoption of "minutes" or statements of policy and belief. Britain Yearly Meeting allows considerable latitude to local meetings but defines itself as "the ultimate authority for church affairs for Quakers in Britain." Some unprogrammed yearly meetings consider their faith and practice "descriptive" with no authority over monthly meetings. Other yearly meetings, especially among evangelical Friends, are more tightly structured with an expectation that individual churches will follow central direction and adhere to doctrine and policy adopted by the yearly meeting. The leaders in such yearly meetings may claim the prerogative to determine how the Bible is interpreted and biblical authority implemented. In the 2010s that tension led to splits in the United States over issues of gender and sexuality. Indiana, North Carolina, and Northwest yearly meetings divided over issues of inclusion and the authority of individual meetings to define themselves as welcoming congregations (see Chapter 7).

THE PRACTICE OF COMMUNITY

Every religious body has to deal with both the practicalities of operating week to week and year to year and the care and nurture of its spiritual life. Apart from the business functions of collecting contributions, paying bills, and maintaining churches and meeting houses, Quakers historically divided responsibilities between groups of "elders" and groups of "overseers" (more on this term later). Elders have been called the guardians of Quakerism since their charge has been to maintain the quality and integrity of worship. Overseers organized and monitored ("oversaw") the life and activities of the community. Among twenty-first-century Friends, each church and meeting parcels out these functions in different assortments of pastors, paid staff, and committees (which have very prominent roles in unprogrammed meetings).

The term "overseer" was firmly established among Friends by the 1700s, when New England Yearly Meeting, for example, required that each meeting choose two "judicious" men and two women as overseers to look after its spiritual welfare. The authoritative *Oxford English Dictionary* includes the following as one of six definitions of overseer: "A person chosen by a church or religious society to serve as a local or regional leader; *spec.* a member of the Religious Society of Friends (Quakers) responsible for the pastoral supervision of a congregation." As a synonym for superintendent, it was well known in England through the position of "overseer of the poor" who administered charity within each church parish. Harvard College has had a board of overseers since the 1640s. As they have struggled to meet the concerns of African American members, however, many US meetings in the twenty-first century have rejected the term because of its historical application to men who often violently controlled enslaved people. "Oversight" committees are now often named as "care and counsel" or "pastoral care" committees.

Pastoral care in its broadest sense is looking after the welfare of members of the meeting or church community—helping families when someone is ill, providing emergency financial assistance, organizing opportunities for socializing, creating opportunities for children to thrive, grow, and become members of the meeting. These functions, of course, are a familiar part of most religious communities. While Friends churches mirror other denominations in placing much of this responsibility on the pastor, unprogrammed meetings, which rarely have paid staff, rely on the care and counsel committee to take the lead in recommendations for marriage and membership, assistance for those in need, memorial services, and similar work.

CLEARNESS AND DISCERNMENT

Modern Quakers have developed the distinctive practice of "clearness committees" to aid individuals in issues of personal discernment. The practice has deeper Quaker antecedents, but the contemporary version developed in the 1960s and 1970s. Clearness committees are a worshipful method for helping an individual through an important life decision that might involve a career change, an educational undertaking, a decision about family matters, or a call to ministry or service. A group of Friends meet with the individual and ask open-ended questions in a worshipful manner, helping the person to reach clarity about the ways in which the divine spirit may be moving in their lives. It is not a bunch of folks offering good advice, but a context in which the individual can explore leadings of the Inward Guide.[2]

Clearness committees are part of the larger process and challenge of discernment among Friends. With no central authority, and each Friend potentially following their own leading, chaos can lurk just around the corner. The short-lived movement of Ranters of the 1650s, for example, had some similar beliefs to Quakers but no group accountability. In what now seems like a quaint phrase, early Quakers worried about "disorderly walkers," meaning people who did what they wanted with little regard for its impact on the group. The spectacular example was James Nayler's re-enactment of Jesus' entry into Jerusalem. His conviction of heresy by the English Parliament threatened the very survival of the new movement (Chapter 2). We might say that very early Quakers superficially resembled the people of Israel before the time of Samuel: "In those days there was no king in Israel. Everyone did what was right in his own eyes" (Judges 21:25). As a result, Quakers find it extremely important that individuals test their ideas and "leadings" for prophetic ministry with the larger community. Such ministry might involve spiritual teaching and writing, expression of artistic talent, organizing for social change, or direct civil disobedience. In every case, discernment is a delicate balance between the individual's direct understanding of their calling or ministry and the wisdom (not authority) of the group. Quaker scholar Ben Pink Dandelion (2010, p. 21) puts it this way:

> So discernment, deciding what is of God and what is not, is the most visible role of the gathered meeting because it is also the most fundamental. It is the most crucial exercise of a church which claims its authority and wisdom is found in a corporate direct encounter over and against text and tradition. The gathered meeting decides for itself what is truly from God ... Our future is in our discernment.

Early Friends identified several criteria for discerning if a leading truly came from God: patience, moral purity, consistency with the Bible, consistency with others, and inward unity. Patience is the most accessible of these tests. It is one of the "fruits of the spirit" listed in Galatians 5:22–23 and an indication of a willingness to leave the results in God's hands. Again, the words from Isaac Penington's 1667 letter to Friends in Chalfont are relevant:

> Life gives [the soul] a feeling, a light, a tasting, an hearing, a smelling, of the heavenly things, by which sense it is able to discern and distinguish them from the earthly. And from this Measure of Life the capacity increases, the senses grow stronger; it sees more, feels more, taste more, hears more, smells more. Now when the senses are grown up to strength ... doubtings and disputes in the mind fly away and the soul lives in the certain demonstration and fresh sense and power of life.

George Fox and others believed that if you are not willing for others to test your leading, it is unlikely to be from God. One can test a leading against scripture, against spiritual writings, or with respected individuals. In current practice, this is likely to involve consultation with a pastor, elders, or a clearness committee. We might translate the concept of moral purity as letting go of one's ego and self-righteousness. Inward unity is sometimes described as peace on a very deep, personal level.

MEMBERSHIP

In the 1700s and 1800s, as the initial fervor lessened, membership increasingly came to be based on family connections as a "birthright Friend." Over the last hundred years, in contrast, the balance has shifted and most members join as adults with no previous connection to Quakers (85 percent in Britain). The congregational basis of Quakerism means that people hold membership in a specific church or monthly meeting, which approves each membership application as a community.

Early Friends talked about a process of "convincement" or "conviction" that was much like a Christian conversion process. When modern unprogrammed Friends use the term "Quaker by convincement" they may mean a more intellectual process of exploration and discovery. Nevertheless, the core of convincement remains the sort of deep mystical experience of that Robert Barclay described for himself. An individual interested in joining an unprogrammed meeting will do reading on their own, attend adult education programs, and meet with a committee that makes sure that membership is a good match on both sides. A Friends church may have regular classes for prospective members, counseling with the pastor, and an expectation that members accept Jesus as Lord. It may also restrict participation of divorced women or individuals who have sex outside a heterosexual marriage. Someone can apply to transfer membership to another local Quaker body, but that church or meeting has to explicitly accept the transfer. This action may be routine in many cases but it would involve discussion and discernment if someone were hoping to transfer, for example, from a liberal Australian meeting to an evangelical North American Friends church. A Friend living in a community for only a few years might ask for a "sojourning membership."

East African Friends recognize different degrees of membership. Just as is the case in many other countries, Chavakali Yearly Meeting in Western Kenya offers junior membership to children. While in most of the world, there is only one category of adult membership, Kenyans have variations related to expectations of responsibility. Chavakali has two levels of primary study—Book 1 and Book 2, each with specific periods of book learning and practice. Book 2 provides a full membership card and is a necessary step before one can serve as clerk or teacher but is not open to men with multiple wives or married women who are not a first wife. The *Faith and Practice* developed in 2002 for Friends United Meeting in East Africa notes that leaders are selected from among those in a monogamous marriage when polygamy is part of the culture.

MINISTRY AND WORSHIP

In addition to the "mechanics" of membership and pastoral care that maintain a church or meeting as an ongoing organization, Quakers take personal responsibility for the quality of worship. From early on they began to designate elders, people with spiritual depth who could monitor and support the spiritual life of the community. Elders in the early centuries often sat on raised "facing benches" from which they could keep an eye on the congregation, variously as nurturing teachers who encouraged individuals with a gift for ministry or as somber disciplinarians (don't fall asleep!). As do most Friends churches, Britain Yearly Meeting retains the practice of naming elders, although it now recognizes that "elders" do not have to be old and is explicit that it is not a hierarchical role.

Unprogrammed meetings in the United States utilize a Committee on Worship and Ministry (or some such name) to serve the same function of caring for the quality of worship. This includes educating people about what works and doesn't work within a particular meeting context. The modern term "weighty Friend" is an informal recognition that a person has particular spiritual depth that they bring to worship. Friends who are disruptive or simply do not understand Quaker worship may find themselves being talked to or "eldered," a term that recalls the old days being called on the carpet by stern old men but that should imply loving and supportive advice.

Early Friends believed that everyone is potentially a minister of the gospel, but they also understood that different people have different abilities and talents and that some individuals were especially effective preachers and teachers through their vocal ministry. The process of formally recognizing or "recording" these individuals by monthly or yearly meetings was systematized in the early 1700s, with the unfortunate result of sometimes inhibiting others from offering vocal ministry in worship. In the early twentieth century, most unprogrammed meetings discontinued the practice for this reason. Programmed meetings continue to record individuals for their spiritual gifts as pastors or as ministers through words or music. Many paid pastors of Friends churches are also recorded ministers, but not all recorded ministers are pastors. Recording, which is a way to recognize spiritual gifts that derive from God and the responsibility to use them well, is different from ordination which gives an individual organizational standing and confers sacredness.

Unprogrammed Friends have filled the gap by identifying "released" Friends. These are individuals with distinct and valued ministries. The term usually means that the person is freed from obligations to serve on meeting committees, and varying amounts of financial support may also be available (to add to the complexity, some programmed meetings speak of paying their pastors as the way to "release" them). The meeting often then creates a support committee or "anchor" committee to advise and support the individual as they pursue their ministry. The work may focus on Quakers through writing and teaching about the Society of Friends or traveling among isolated Friends, or it may involve bringing a spiritual dimension to work on minority rights, the inequities and iniquity of capital punishment, or the challenges that individuals face at the end of their lives.

SACRAMENTS AND SACRAMENTAL LIVES

Pastoral work among Friends has the same goals as in other denominations, but anyone accustomed to standard Christian practice will also find a glaring absence in Quaker meetings and churches. Since their earliest years, Quakers have considered the formal, public sacraments of baptism and communion to be unnecessary. There is no weekly ritual of mass, no milestones like first communion and water baptism to signal confirmation or conversion to church membership. For mainstream Christians, these two practices are visible signs that communicate and reaffirm God's presence. Early Friends, however, believed that God communicates directly with each individual and with individuals in community, and expected to experience the inward baptism of the Holy Spirit. George Fox described his encounter with a group of Baptists:

> And one of them said that what was not of faith was sin. Whereupon I asked them what faith was, and how it was wrought in man. But they turned off from that and spoke of their baptism in water. Then I asked them whether their mountain of sin was brought down and laid low in them, and their rough and crooked ways made smooth and straight in them, for they looked upon the Scriptures as meaning outward mountains and way. But I told them they must find them in their own hearts; which they seemed to wonder at.
>
> (Fox 1952, p. 45)

The communal sharing of the divine presence that is enacted in many churches by the formal sacrament of communion is experienced by Friends in a "gathered" meeting in which those present experience deep inner quiet and a sense of the shared presences of the divine. Both unprogrammed and evangelical Friends continue to share this belief. As Northwest Yearly Meeting of Friends Church put it in their *Faith and Practice*:

> We believe Christ's baptism to be the inward receiving of the promised Holy Spirit, whereby the believer is immersed in Jesus' power, purity, and wisdom. This baptism is the essential Christian baptism: an experience of cleansing from sin that supplants old covenant rituals. The sanctification that is initiated with this experience is a continuing work of the Holy Spirit.

WORSHIP SHARING

Worship sharing is a distinctive community building practice that emerged out of the social activism of the 1950s and 1960s. It has been one of the ways in which more liberal Quakers have tried to reinvigorate their faith and practice. The key figure was teacher and civil rights activist Rachel Davis DuBois, who developed a method for intercultural conversations and adapted it to the Quaker context as a method of group introspection. Worship sharing as practiced since the 1970s is a relaxed and structured version of meeting for worship. A small group gathers in a circle and a facilitator offers a question for reflection. Each person speaks as they are moved, but only once and directly from their own experience rather than pontificating or responding to someone else. It is meant to be a safe and confidential space for sharing, not a forum for discussion and argument. An ideal worship-sharing session simultaneously strengthens community through non-judgmental sharing and draws participants into worshipful consideration and reflection on aspects of their lives.

SPECIAL MEETINGS FOR WORSHIP

Quakers have a distinctive approach to the ceremony of marriage. Again, because the divine is accessible to all, Friends historically have considered marriage as a covenant between two people and God. Family and friends in attendance serve as witnesses. The simplicity of the ceremony among early Friends dispensed with the formal ritual laid out in the *Book of Common Prayer* of the Church of England As George Fox rather firmly put it in 1669, "right joining in marriage is the work of the Lord only, and not the priests' or magistrates'; for it is God's ordinance and not man's ... we marry none; it is the Lord's work and we are but witnesses." Although other Christian churches also recognize the special character of marriage as essentially a covenant relationship, the traditional Quaker marriage ceremonies continue to stand out for simplicity and the absence of an officiating minister or priest who formally recognizes the union. In Kenya, customary marriage is recognized as legal, but in Friends churches members are urged to exchange vows in church. This step is necessary for full membership and for those in leadership.

In practice, most unprogrammed and many Northern Hemisphere programmed meetings take marriages under their care after a clearness process. Originally this was to assure that a couple were legally free to marry. The ceremony itself may take place in a meetinghouse or church, a community center, or a park. Friends churches may have pastors who preside over the marriage, but in the more traditional form the couple stand amid the worshipping community to speak their vows to each other. They then sign a certificate which notes the date and place, includes the vows, and has room for everyone in attendance to sign in witness. Couples may write their own vows, but these are usually a variation or updating of standard language to be said by each with the appropriate insertions and changes: "In the presence of God, and these our friends, I take you A.B. to be my wife [or you C.D to be my husband], promising with divine assistance to be unto you a loving and faithful husband/wife, as long as we both shall live." The meeting clerk or pastor fills out the paperwork to satisfy the authorities and the couple take the signed certificate home to hang on their wall as a reminder that Quakerism is both a do-it-yourself religion and a practice of community.

Kenyan Friends recognize the need for divine intervention when human strength fails and believe that Christ is just as willing to heal the sick now as when he lived on earth. Thus, they conduct worship services focused on prayer for healing for the sick or those otherwise in need. They also pray for guidance for those about to travel and gratitude for their return.

In many Quaker communities, particularly the unprogrammed ones, memorial meetings for worship are similar to a normal Sunday gathering, but with some simple additions. Normally, as people enter, they are given a small pamphlet with information on the life of the deceased Friend as well as directions on what to expect. Music may be played as individuals are asked to enter the meeting room in silence. When all have gathered, a designated person will rise and describe Quaker worship for those who have never attended meeting. After a few minutes of silent worship someone will stand and share reflections on the life of the deceased. The remainder of the time is in worshipful silence with an expectation that anyone present may offer reflections on this individual and their place in the community.

BEYOND MAJORITY RULE: QUAKER DECISION-MAKING

The deeply personal character of Quaker worship and Quaker belief in the immediate accessibility of the Inward Light to those who are open have always raised organizational problems. Ever since George Fox and Margaret Fell asserted the need for structure and discipline within the new movement, individuals have chafed at what they see as deadening restrictions. Others see the same forms—business practice, clearness committees, eldering, individual and group discernment—as guides to help channel spiritual gifts and support prophetic leadership. The creative tension is central to the Quaker experience.

A stranger who drops in on a North American Quaker meeting for business may first think that they are in the familiar territory of an annual membership meeting of a nonprofit organization. There will be a printed or posted agenda, a gathering that may number dozens or hundreds, a couple of people up front to take notes and manage the discussion, and committee reports on familiar topics like the annual budget, property maintenance, and social service projects. Participants make comments and sometimes argue alternative positions. But the visitor also begins to notice that something—several things—are missing. Nobody seconds a motion because nobody makes a motion to start discussion. Decisions happen mysteriously without a count of ayes and nays, but with clear agreement from the group. Any reference to *Robert's Rules of Order* is quite out of order. Depending on local custom, participation may be limited to formal members or open to anyone who wishes to attend.

The visitor is witnessing a very distinctive decision-making process. It results in agreement by everyone in the room, or nearly everyone, but it is not majority rule. The discussion and resulting agreement looks superficially like a secular consensus process, but it has a radically different foundation. As commonly understood, consensus is a "political" process that often involves negotiation and compromise to identify a common center. Quaker business meeting, in contrast, is ideally a spiritual practice. Friends approach important questions in the expectation that shared worshipful seeking will enable the group to reach a divinely guided under-standing or unity that is often called the "sense of the meeting." Janet Scott puts it this way: "Business meetings reflect the faith that the primary authority is that of God; as the God whose will is sought; as Christ who presides; and as the Holt Spirit who inspires and empowers. Thus the task of the meeting is to listen in worship under that authority, to discern the right way forward on any piece of business" (Abbott, et al., 2012, p. 57).

"Sense of the meeting" is a sometimes confusing phrase. It ide-ally reflects unanimous agreement by all present as to the leading of the Holy Spirit. Only rarely does a Quaker group proceed without complete agreement and then only after careful consideration over several weeks or months. This consideration may involve informational sessions, small group discussion, and "threshing ses-sions" where multiple voices are heard, but with no attempt to reach a decision. Only then is the church ready to decide impor-tant questions—whether to remodel the current building or look for new property, how to deal with a large and unexpected financial windfall, when to make public statements on their rela-tions with the broader culture such as opposition to war or how (or whether) to welcome people of all sexual orientations and gender identities. Sometimes the decision coalesces unexpectedly, as if a kaleidoscope has been twirled and the pieces have fallen into a clear pattern that is satisfying to the large majority. In some cases, an individual who continues to disagree with a decision may ask to be formally noted or minuted as "standing aside" from the decision—in effect abstaining publicly. If someone continues to look through the kaleidoscope and is unable to see the pattern, the group may with reluctance move ahead anyway.

There are some norms that Friends try to follow with the hope that individuals can lay aside their own agendas and preconceptions and be open to divine guidance. Individuals should only speak once, unless they find they have something very new to say. They should address the presiding clerk and definitely refrain from debating someone with a different view or approach. Liberal Friends refrain from voting on an issue because it can polarize and divide, reducing even a relatively non-controversial issue to a question with two separate sides and no middle options. Many Friends in Latin America and some North American evangelical Friends do vote on some occasions, however, reflecting cultural differences.

The distinctiveness of Quaker decision making is seen in the roles of the clerk and recording clerk, the Quaker names for what look like the presiding officer and secretary. The clerk of a monthly or yearly meeting is the servant of the meeting. They often are the public face or contact person, and have the responsibility to structure agendas for business meetings and manage discussion. The essential task, however, is to pay attention to emerging agreement and to help crystalize the discussion, while the recording clerk (an American innovation) assists and helps to put emerging agreement into words. The clerk is not a gavel-wielding chairperson but a listener who makes sure that all ideas and responses are heard but that no few individuals dominate. A clerk who wants to contribute directly to a discussion literally "stands aside" by stepping away from the clerking table to speak as an individual. As a meeting continues, the presiding clerk may try to articulate what seems to be the common ground or agreement and let the gathering test that against their own sense. After some trial and error, the clerking team crafts a minute or summary statement on which the group agrees. Important decisions are often considered at one meeting and held over to the next, a process sometimes called seasoning, on analogy to newly cut wood that is seasoned for a time before it is ready for the fireplace or the fine piece of furniture.

Friends use the term "minute" in two ways. The minutes of a business meeting are like the minutes of other organizations, including a notation of committee reports and decisions on everything from buying new carpeting to accepting a new member. Meetings also minute or note births, marriages, and deaths in their formal record. In addition, meetings sometimes create formal statements of their positions on public issues, such as a minute on nuclear disarmament or minute on capital punishment, which they then publicize in an effort to influence public opinion and policy.

Because of the assumption that business decisions should be made by the group under divine guidance, there is no proxy voting. Friends must show up to be part of the process. At the same time, it is vital to provide ample opportunities for participation and input when issues are controversial and divisive. Beyond prosaic but messy personality conflicts, such issues fall into three broad categories:

- One is whether to make statements on public issues like criminal justice reform, which often involve protracted debates over wording even when there is basic agreement about the underlying issues.
- A second category is money and property. There is nothing like a large bequest or a proposal to raise money for a larger building to surface deep differences about how to live the testimony of simplicity. Some argue that a well-funded church or meeting with an attractive building can be more effective in serving the larger community and others advocate for what we might call organizational voluntary poverty and critics might call shabbiness.
- In the third category are questions of individual and community morality that frequently divide religious bodies. Slavery in the eighteenth century, evolution and temperance in the nineteenth century, and the acceptable parameters of gender identity and sexual orientation more recently have posed challenges to the testimony of equality and understanding of the Bible. On these and similar issues, Quakers have often taken leading progressive positions, but not always unanimously and always after struggles to balance moral imperatives with the default assumptions of their larger society.

The common theme for this chapter can be summarized in a single sentence. The centrality of the worshipping and worshipful community is the foundation for the Quaker approach to both group and individual decisions. Friends believe that personal insight and prophetic ministry are most powerful when tested with the group, allowing individuals to understand their own spiritual experience in and through the experience of others on the same journey. The practice of discernment, which thoughtful Friends repeatedly place at the heart of Quaker testimony, is not simply checking in with the church authorities to get a green light. It is a consultation with and willingness to consider the wisdom of others. As Jay O'Hara has put it, Friends need a community to help separate truth from empty rhetoric (he uses a more colorful term) and to support their calling. In other words, what looks superficially like a "do-it-yourself" religion is more accurately a "do-it-ourselves" religion—a community of seekers and believers working together under the guidance of a higher spirit which many Friends name the Light of Christ.

NOTES

1 It is reported that Haverford College students took wagers on the highly predictable moment when the influential theologian Rufus Jones would rise to speak at campus meeting for worship.
2 The Quaker clearness committee has no connection to the concept of being "Clear" in Scientology.

FURTHER READING

Michael Birkel, *Silence and Witness* (Maryknoll, NY: Orbis Books, 2004). The history and practical dimensions of Quaker spirituality.

Howard Brinton, *A Guide to Quaker Practice* (Wallingford, PA: Pendle Hill Publications, 1942; 4e 2006). An operating manual for unprogrammed Friends.

Ben Pink Dandelion, *Celebrating the Quaker Way* (London: Quaker Books, 2010). A pocket-sized summary of the spirit of liberal Quakerism.

Parker J. Palmer, *A Hidden Wholeness: The Journey Toward an Undivided Life* (San Francisco, CA: Jossey-Bass, 2009). A noted author and teacher translates Quaker practice for non-Quakers.

John Punshon, *Encounter with Silence: Reflections from the Quaker Tradition* (Richmond, IN: Friends United Press, 1987). A deeply personal exploration of Quaker faith and practice by a British Friend.

Jack L. Willcuts, *Why Friends Are Friends* (Newberg, OR: Barclay Press, 1984). An evangelical Quaker that places faith and practice within the biblical context familiar to early Friends.

MINISTRY, MISSION, AND TESTIMONY

> And then was the time of his Love, even when he stood at the Door
> of our Hearts and knockt, that he might be entertained by us; yes,
> and sometimes in the silence of the Night hath he broken in upon us;
> I know it in my own particular, when no Creature hath been near, this
> Invisible Oracle hath secretly communed with me, reproving me,
> wherein I had done amiss; and showing me what was right in his
> Sight. And at other times in Company, thus would the Lord cause his
> Voice to sound in my Heart [The Customs of the People are Vain] by
> which I was brought off from many of those Vanities which before I
> had spent time in; and that by the Witness of God in my own
> Conscience, which testified against the same.
>
> (Elizabeth Bathurst, *Truth Vindicated*, 1695)

Awareness that the Holy Spirit was shaping their lives led early
Friends like Elizabeth Bathurst to recognize each other as prophets
who listened inwardly for holy guidance. The modern Conservative Friend William Taber, in his pamphlet "The Prophetic
Stream," named three characteristics of the prophetic ministry:
daily and even minute-to-minute inward attention to God, living
consistently with the teachings of Jesus, and helping to draw others
into divine love. We can also describe Quakers as "everyday prophets" who may sometimes be called to take bold public stances
against injustice, but who also seek to live out the call in Micah 6:8
to love mercy and walk humbly with God in the ordinary
interactions of their lives.

Modern Friends often speak of their faith in terms of *testimony*,
or the way their lives serve as expressions of their faith, although

different traditions use the concept differently. Unprogrammed, liberal Friends regularly point to their peace testimony, efforts to live simply, and other behaviors as a centrally defining aspect of Quakerism. Evangelical friends often focus on testifying to the work of Jesus Christ in their hearts that transforms them so their lives manifest the fruits of the Spirit. These are different emphases rather than distinct meanings. All Friends draw on a heritage in which prompts for action and for everyday life arise out of worship and transforming attention to the Inward Guide. Whether a Friend names that Guide Jesus Christ or the Pure Principle of love and truth, it opens awareness of the demands of social justice and proclaims a way of life that communicates a vision of the kingdom of God on earth. Distinctive Quaker practices have changed over the years, even as they sustain a continuing core meaning that testifies to eternal truths. For instance, the longstanding requirement for plain dress has been refocused to relate more directly to John Woolman's admonition to witness against the causes of war in greed and accumulation of wealth. This chapter returns to the topics introduced in Chapter 1 and places them in theological as well as political context, exploring the ways in which the social witness of Friends can be seen as distinctive.

THE "SPICES"

Friends testimonies convey an "outward sign and witness to an inward spiritual leading," in the words of Quaker scholar Wilmer Cooper (1990, p. 157). These broad truths are expressed in distinctive ways varying over time and cultures. Cooper identifies four *religious* testimonies: belief that individuals have direct access to God's leadings for their words and actions; awareness that individuals and groups might act in accord with that knowledge; identification of the church as the gathered fellowship of worshippers; and belief that all of life can be sacred so that the outward life reflects the inward life of the Spirit. He then goes on to speak of what he calls "the social testimonies," which are often expressed today simply as the testimonies or as the "SPICES." Widely accepted practices are often named as "Quaker distinctives" by modern evangelical Friends.

In the eighteenth and nineteenth centuries (see Chapter 3) the testimonies could seem constraining rather than liberating. Historian Thomas Hamm describes how testimonies that ruled Friends' lives in past centuries not only included opposition to slavery and warfare, but also to frivolous and profane literature, worldly diversions, music, and a "hireling ministry" (Quaker talk for paid clergy) that they saw as distracting from the work of the Spirit. In short, several generations of Quakers set themselves in opposition to what they conceived as "the world." Their lives were proscribed by the "discipline," a "thin dreary volume" that regulated every aspect of life, from the width of hat brims to the height of gravestones. Overseers enforced the regulations, a group whom one disgruntled birthright Friend described in 1910 as a cross between medieval inquisitors and modern detectives. Disownment, which removed an offending Friend from membership after considerable discussion but allowed them to continue to join in worship, is almost unknown in the past century with the exception of unrepenting child abuse.

In contrast to this rather bleak history, twentieth- and twenty-first-century Quakers have reinvigorated the idea that testimonies are a central and positive part of practice and belief. Indeed, they are often the reason individuals seek out Quaker meetings and churches. Although all evangelicals may not use this terminology, most Friends accept the SPICES—simplicity, peace, integrity, community, equality, and stewardship—as basic guidance for how to live.

Quaker teacher and writer Howard Brinton coined the acronym in the 1950s, initially including only simplicity, peace, community, and equality. The shorthand has proved a convenient and flexible summary for many modern Quakers, but there has always been fluidity in naming the central witnesses that identify the Religious Society of Friends. Some yearly meetings may emphasize social justice or sustainability and care for the earth in addition to non-violence and affirming the presence of God in every heart. Concern for all people and their well-being flows through the testimonies in a way that echoes Jesus' Sermon on the Mount and the epistle of James.

Members of the Religious Society of Friends have always engaged the larger world as public ministers, not only by the words they speak during worship but also by their actions in bringing the testimonies to life in distinctive behaviors. Ministry has a particular meaning among Friends, growing out of the original expectation that everyone can attend to God's call in their own lives. Someone might be called to speak during the expectant silence of open worship. Another might be called to travel to Africa to train village medical workers. In contemporary Friends churches, such individuals may be released from the need to hold a secular job by being hired as pastors. The congregation may also recognize ministers in the congregation who are not pastors, but who speak regularly in open worship or have a ministry of teaching.

The absence of a permanent paid ministry, as found among early Friends and modern unprogrammed Friends, is unusual. Christianity often distinguishes between the clergy and the laity. Friends have at times explained themselves by saying that early Friends abolished the laity as a category because everyone is potentially a minister without requiring academic degrees or ordination. At the same time, Meetings have since almost their first days recorded the names of individuals who had a gift in the vocal ministry and provided them with letters endorsing their gifts when they were moved to travel with their message.

Individuals who have experienced a call to travel in the ministry have knit together the Religious Society of Friends from the beginning. Margaret Fell and others coordinated much of the earliest travel, encouraging ministers to visit new meetings that might benefit from their spiritual depth and experience. An individual would notice an inward drawing to go to a certain region or group of meetings. A few even wrote in their journals that they sat in their carriage at a fork in the road waiting to feel drawn in a particular direction. These Friends depended on local Quakers to host them, although their home meeting might provide needed expenses or arrange for someone to care for their family or a farm while they were traveling. Sometimes a visiting Friend might sit at the front of the meeting waiting and listening for a message to share only to find that they had no words, choosing to stay silent rather than offering a prepared message. Sometimes they would note a feeling that those present were not ready to receive the message they had brought.

Travel in the ministry with the blessings of one's home community has continued to the present. It may follow the traditional practice, but can take several distinct forms. Some Friends feel a personal call and travel as individuals to bring peacebuilding skills, to teach tools for healing in the aftermath of conflict, to accompany local people in the face of violence, and to work in other ways to build a more peaceful and just world. Travel is often initiated by yearly meetings or other Quaker organizations that invite individuals to speak on particular topics relating to spirituality, faith, testimonies, or Quaker practice. The organizations may also sponsor individuals on worship and speaking tours. Members of Friends churches may also travel as missionaries who expect to settle for an extended period in a different country in order to teach new skills and education and to bring people to salvation through Christ.

SIMPLICITY AND PLAINNESS

Plainness is both a theological and social concept for Friends. The 1993 *Faith and Practice* of North Pacific Yearly Meeting asks, "Do we center our lives in the awareness of the presence of God so that all things take their rightful place?" Early Friends lived and acted simply in order to remove anything that fostered pride or distracted from the relationship between self and God, be it wealth, striving after success, or fashionable dress. As Emma Lapsansky (2003, p. 4) has phrased it, the imperative was to "dampen the noise of everyday life" in order to be open to the voice of the Inward Christ. Meeting places were not to be ornamented with crosses, stained-glass windows, or decorations that might substitute aesthetic pleasure for religious experience. Friends saw church ritual as a distraction and money spent on "steeple houses" as irrelevant to living out the kingdom of God. William Penn argued for plain living by asserting that the production of luxury goods impoverished the realm by making wealth more unequal. However, during the eighteenth century, the theologically radical plainness of early Quakerism had become as much a tool for maintaining a distinct outward identity of the group as a spiritual practice.

In meetinghouses as well as in clothing and furniture, the Quaker style that evolved in the eighteenth and nineteenth centuries did not require the absolute austerity that early Quaker *plainness* might seem to have implied. Quakers lived in the world,

some with substantial financial success, and emphasized craftsman-
ship over fashion, sparseness over ornamentation, elegance over
sumptuousness. In meetinghouses built by post-pioneer generations, the result was often simple lines but elegant materials and
finish. "Quaker Plain Style" is a standard architectural term in
the United States, used in nominations to the National Register
of Historic Places. Reaching back to Quaker origins is the belief
that any place will do for worship. Friends may gather for worship in recycled factories, converted houses, community centers,
under spreading trees, and in surplus school rooms as well as
purpose-built structures.

Simplicity can be a political as well as a spiritual choice. To use a
pre-existing space is to free resources for other purposes. To worship in a venerable structure is to conserve the built environment
while appreciating clean, spare meeting rooms. When Friends
remodel or build new meetinghouses, they may utilize new materials but often choose to recapitulate the spare forms and horizontal
lines of older buildings. In addition, there is a strong emphasis on
abundant natural light. Indeed, *bright natural light* has become a
guiding principle of many newer meetinghouses. Natural light
represents conservation of resources, substitutes the play of sunbeam
and shadow for manufactured decoration, and metaphorically
reenacts the inward light of the divine.

Three striking examples are new meetinghouses designed in
collaboration with James Turrell, a visual artist who grew up
Quaker. He is noted for large-scale installations that manipulate
and dramatize light. Live Oak Meetinghouse in Houston, completed in 2000, centers its meeting room under a "sky space" that
brings simple natural or monochromatic light into the space of
worship. In Turrell's words, he was "very interested in this literal
look at it—actually greeting this light that you find in meditation,
and following that" (https://art21.org/read/james-turrell-live-oa
k-friends-meeting-house/). Chestnut Hill Meetinghouse in
Philadelphia was rebuilt in 2013 with another version of a Turrell
light-space. The next year, Britain Yearly Meeting completed
renovations at Friends House in London that added a skylight and
tiered ceiling to the main meeting room. The aesthetic stands in
full contrast to Gothic cathedrals and their imitations, with their

complex forms, verticality, high spaces, ambient darkness, and intricate stained-glass windows.

What about an office building? Can it support spiritual values and spiritual journeys in ways that parallel the spiritual work of cathedrals and temples? Friends Committee on National Legislation (FCNL) is the organization that American Friends established to lobby Congress. FCNL's leadership certainly believe that the renovation of its Washington, D.C. building in 2005 with a deep concern for its impact on the earth is "a manifestation of the practice of faith," both by its location and its expression of belief in the unity of creation (see Chapter 1). The Quaker approach overlaps with broader political and environmental movements, but Friends seek to differentiate themselves in insisting that action be spiritually grounded.

PEACE: CHALLENGING THE ROOTS OF WAR

George Fox (1952, p. 65) declared, "I lived in the virtue of that life and power that took away the occasion of all wars, and I knew from whence all wars did rise, from the lust according to James doctrine." He was referring to the Epistle of James 4:1: "These conflicts and disputes among you, where do they come from? Do they not come from your cravings that are at war within you?" Fox was rejecting the promise of release from prison in 1651 if he would take up a commission in Cromwell's New Model Army to fight for establishment of the kingdom of God on earth. This was one of many statements of Quaker refusal to take up arms, even to achieve goals they agreed with. It took another decade for Friends as a group to consistently make formal statements that refusal to participate in war was one of their testimonies to the world.

The peace testimony was most clearly a witness against participation in wars and taking up arms. It was strict enough that fighting in the American Revolution for either side, profiting from the war, or otherwise supporting it in any way were all disownable offenses, meaning that someone was barred from attending business meeting or speaking on behalf of Friends. Disowned individuals could still participate in worship and other aspects of community life. However, the peace testimony came into direct conflict with the abhorrence of slavery during the American Civil War. Few

Meetings were willing to disown those who fought to end slavery. Nonetheless, yearly meeting books of discipline spoke of the evangelical promise to learn war no more, following Christ's example, and sometimes condemned war outright as non-Christian.

World War I, which required massive military conscription in Britain and the United States, brought new urgency to the peace testimony. That ferocious conflict again posed the choice of remaining true to Quaker pacifism or joining what many considered a war to save democracy. Many young Quakers requested exemption because of their religiously based and conscientious objection to war. Perhaps a third of male Friends of military age in Britain enlisted. Their meetings usually accepted the choice unless they explicitly disavowed the peace testimony. Other young Quakers refused to serve, risking imprisonment while the Quaker community lobbied to establish legal recognition for conscientious objector (CO) status. At the same time, British Friends took direct action to relieve suffering with the Friends Ambulance Unit which deployed volunteers beginning in 1914. Substantial famine relief programs in war-torn Europe after 1918 became the widely known hallmarks of Quaker practice.

This "war-abolishing Quaker Peace Testimony" has expanded to embrace a "conflict-transforming Peace Testimony," in the formulation of Canadian Friend Elaine Bishop and Korean Friend Jisok Jung. What for many years was primarily a testimony against war can be better understood in the twenty-first century as a witness for peace in all aspects of life. For example, Quaker sociologist Elise Boulding (1989) argued that the home is the learning ground for developing peaceful means to respond to conflict. Individual transformation is part of this work and teaches lessons that can be brought to bear in a wide variety of situations, thus giving tools to work on the root causes of violence and war.

Friends are increasingly putting their energies into developing broader perspectives on the nature of peace, differentiating between peace enforced by coercion as in repressive societies (sometimes called "false peace" or "unpeace") and peace as a process that requires attention to economic and social justice as well as human dignity. This second understanding is what Adam Curle (1981) calls a state of living justly before God—a state more akin to George Fox's declaration to take away the occasion for war.

Bishop and Jung see reconciliation as an essential part of creating a true peace: "Taking away the occasion for war requires more than righting unjust situations. It requires addressing the damage done during conflict … Reconciliation does not come easily. It requires persistence and time. It is based on a shared respect for a shared humanity." This only hints at the complexity they see in the conflict-transforming dimension of the peace testimony (Bishop and Jung, in Angell and Dandelion, 2018, pp. 118, 119)

Cultures of peace, both Quaker and non-Quaker, include respect for individual dignity and human rights, a permanent ban on all weapons of mass destruction, eradication of poverty, and a strong global environmental protection agency protected by both governments and civil society. Evangelical Quaker Ron Mock argues that Christians must love their enemies and must ground their responses to terrorism and tyranny in love. He describes sources of terrorism in political misery leading to corrosive grievance and dehumanizing hatred that can result in belief in the myth of effective violence. He advocates enabling Christians to love in the face of terrorism and tyranny.

The evolution of the peace testimony from a personal stance to efforts to prevent war and care for its victims has sat well with nearly all Friends. The argument that there can be no peace without justice—without efforts to remove the social, economic, and political inequalities that lead to conflict—has been more troubling. Theologically liberal meetings in Britain or the United States can sometimes feel like extensions of left-leaning political parties with no place for alternative voices, and meetings for worship can occasionally devolve into discussion sessions on the latest issue of the *Guardian* or *New York Times*. The deeper challenge is that social justice work may lead individuals or Quaker organizations to cooperate with groups that do not act from a religious foundation and that may accept violent or revolutionary tactics. Friends debate whether to participate in demonstrations and actions where the message of non-violent protest may be swamped by militant action (for example, protests against the World Trade Organization in Seattle and Genoa). Peace and justice work in places like South Africa during apartheid or in Israel/Palestine brings this tension center stage. In the United States, these issues have reinforced the distance between liberal and evangelical Friends.

Evangelical Friends understand their peace work within the Christian tradition of historic Quakerism, and proclaiming the Prince of Peace as one's savior remains central for many Friends. Friends churches place individual salvation at the heart of Christianity, but are more apt than fellow evangelicals to value peacemaking and opposition to war. Many evangelical Quakers work side by side with liberal Quakers in organizations such as Friends Committee on National Legislation. However, the most fundamentalist Friends resist cooperation with their more liberal counterparts as "unequal yoking" that subordinates the search for Christ to secondary secular needs, even if otherwise they might agree on the need to oppose war, house refugees, and promote economic development. Yet even as these Friends have made establishment of missions around the world a primary focus, social justice work is often an important component along with care for individual souls. According to Esther Mombo and Cécile Nyiramana (2016, p. 10), "as Quakers we embark on peacebuilding to help reconcile people to God, to their neighbors and to nature. Our work begins with dealing with the hurt at the individual level, and also healing at all levels of society for lasting peace."

Both Friends United Meeting and Evangelical Friends Church International would point to the centrality in their lives of the Great Commission as stated in Matthew 28:19–20. In that passage Jesus says to his disciples: "Therefore go and make disciples of all nations, baptizing them in the name of the Father and of the Son and of the Holy Spirit, and teaching them to obey everything I have commanded you." A theology of reconciliation is integral to much of this Quaker mission work. It cuts across cultural and political divisions in countries such as Rwanda and Burundi struggling through genocide and civil war. As described in Chapter 1 and Chapter 4, healing and rebuilding community has been a hallmark of Quakers in these lands. In Central and South America the outreach has been predominantly towards indigenous and marginalized people by providing education, health care, and other necessities as integral to the gospel message.

INTEGRITY: HONESTY AND WHOLENESS

When Marge was sworn in as a member of the Oregon Ocean Policy Advisory Council in 1992, Governor Barbara Roberts knew enough about Quakers to ask Marge to affirm that what she said was true rather than following the customary practice of swearing on a scared book. Friends assert that in addition to honoring the command of Jesus to swear not at all, taking an oath implies that normally individuals are not honest in their words and deeds.

Cultural pressures shape how many see integrity. Politics seem to be rife with deliberate falsehoods and the media are full of misinformation. As noted previously, early Friends became widely known for honesty in business dealings. Quaker-owned stores were known for neither bargaining with nor cheating customers. In the twentieth century, Quaker economist Kenneth Boulding rethought the basics of economics by melding scientific inquiry with moral vision. This led him to develop approaches that addressed crucial issues such as environmental and ecological problems by drawing on Christian ethical assumptions. Today's Friends retain the concern for truth-telling, but have not, perhaps because of their tiny numbers, become a symbol for honesty, except in parts of Africa and Latin America where they are an important source of government employees.

But even more than a concern for truth-telling, the Quaker sense of integrity grows out of their doctrine of perfection and belief that it is possible for humans to live without sin. Jesus commanded people to "be ye perfect therefore even as your Father in heaven is perfect," clearly using the meaning of the Greek word translated as perfection as one of coming into completeness or wholeness (Matthew 5:48). Kenyan Friend Oliver Kisaka Simiyu (2001, p. 10) expresses it this way: "Integrity as all people know and desire it begins with a wholesome approach to life. Humanity's complete being—spirit, soul and heart—need to be in harmony … Integrity is consistency, honesty, trustworthiness, dependability and wholesomeness." He goes on to speak of the ways in which faith is strengthened as people attend to God's leadings and that with this faith each person has the capacity to "stand on the truth even in the face of adversity." Sustained by prayer, such integrity shapes individuals dedicated to the service of God and acting in truth no matter the pressures to do otherwise.

Truth-telling and accountability in the handling of money is a critical issue everywhere, but African Friends are especially concerned to be a force against corruption They point out the powerful negative economic and social forces that they face, citing Transparency International's corruption perception index for 2015 which placed Kenya, Uganda, Democratic Republic of the Congo, and Burundi among the world's more corrupt countries. Society-wide corruption has the potential to negatively impact almost every aspect of the social fabric. Kenyan Friends are among those who have stepped forward to make honesty and integrity a priority.

Similarly, Rwandan Friend David Bucura (2013, pp. 9, 18) reminds us that integrity is central to Quaker thought and practice, calling for authenticity and faithfulness in conscience illumined by the Light Within. He agrees with scholar Wilmer Cooper that integrity reaches beyond simple truth-telling, but is a way of being which reflects wholeness of God's truth and "God's way for individuals and groups to function in ways that build the kingdom of God and strengthen believers." He points out that loyalty to family and kin is one of the highest values in his culture in contrast to European and North American individualism. Family ties become doubly important in countries where there is little in the way of public social services and individuals with jobs are expected to share their wealth to cover school fees or health-care costs of others in their clan. Bucura writes:

> This brings us to the dilemmas that can stretch our understandings of Biblical standards of integrity. Suppose there is a believer who has been appointed to serve as treasurer of their church and has been given strict standards of accountability for the funds given to do the Lord's work. What do they do with the pressure they may receive from their community of kin groups to "loan" some of the church funds to meet an urgent need? Are they prepared to insist that the needs of the church take precedence over those of one's extended family?

COMMUNITY: ORGANIZING FOR SOCIAL AND POLITICAL CHANGE

Interdependence is an important dimension of Quaker faith, the conduct of business, and witness in the world. Community and joint action is also a central dimension of Quaker work to challenge injustice. Friends have established formal organizations to support and amplify individual ministry for social betterment.

Many nineteenth-century Quakers who instigated, participated, and shaped social change joined in broader movements for women's rights, abolition of slavery, peace, and prohibition of alcohol sales rather than organizing explicitly as Quakers. When monthly and yearly meetings spun their wheels, arguing among themselves over theology and organizational differences, Quaker activists looked for allies. The result was powerful but somewhat diffuse influence as reform-minded Quakers built coalitions and worked with people from many religious and secular backgrounds. This pattern continued in the twentieth century. Quakers have been founders or key figures in a wide range of progressive and human rights organizations such as the American Civil Liberties Union, Amnesty International, Fellowship of Reconciliation, OXFAM, and Greenpeace. The goals of these organizations are compatible with the hopes and aspirations of many Friends, but they operate with secular rather than Quaker decision-making practice.

A shift toward more explicitly *Quaker* social action in the United States came with American entry into World War I. Only weeks after the United States declared war on Germany and its allies in April 1917, leading Quakers organized the American Friends Service Committee to provide opportunities for humanitarian service for draft-age Friends who objected to participating in the military. The new organization explicitly balanced pacifism and patriotism, stating that "we offer our services to the Government of the United States in any constructive work in which we can conscientiously serve humanity" (Frost 1992, p. 9). AFSC initially sent young men to work with war refugees behind Allied lines. It cooperated with other peace churches and with British Friends who already had war relief experience through the Friends Ambulance Unit. From its start AFSC downplayed explicit theology to avoid differences among Friends, stressing a testimony of service in action. Friends in Canada organized the similar Canadian Friends Service Committee in 1931.

In the following decades, AFSC's most conspicuous activity was relief work with the victims of war. That work has crossed or ignored political borders and divisions that limit direct government efforts. In the early 1920s, the American government asked AFSC to undertake a massive food relief program in defeated Germany, which it extended into Eastern Europe and the Soviet Union (whose communist regime was actively opposed by the United States). It acquired a strong reputation for humanitarian work without political strings or religious proselytizing. The same even-handed approach marked its work during the Spanish Civil War of 1936–9 and in politically divided China during the late 1940s. In Vietnam it operated a child care and rehab center in Quang Ngai in South Vietnam but also sent medical aid to North Vietnam. Large-scale relief efforts in Europe after World War II, which mirrored those after the war of 1914–18, earned Friends the 1947 Nobel Prize for Peace, jointly accepted on behalf of all Quakers by AFSC and Britain's Friends Service Council. Individual Quakers have also received the Nobel Peace Prize—Emily Green Balch in 1946 as a founder of the Women's International League for Peace and Freedom and Philip Noel-Baker in 1959 for his work for nuclear disarmament.

During World War II British Friends reconstituted the Friends Ambulance Unit. The American Friends Service Committee worked with the Mennonites and Church of the Brethren, the other historic peace churches, to organize and operate Civilian Public Service camps for conscientious objectors to military service, who came from all flavors of Quakerism. AFSC worked to miti-gate the impact of the forced removal of 112,000 Japanese Americans from four western states by the federal government in 1942. AFSC workers and volunteers helped many Japanese Americans to relocate to jobs and schools outside the zone from which they were banned and thus avoid incarceration in bleak internment camps. They also helped Japanese American families reestablish themselves after the war.

Individual Quakers, local meetings, and the AFSC continued to work against racial discrimination after 1945. Motivated by pro-gressive politics and by the principle of integrity, many Friends tried to act consistently on their beliefs. The small number of Quakers meant that the efforts were often small in scale. For example, a single meeting outside Philadelphia defended a local librarian against dismissal for left-wing views. AFSC staff worked with individual companies to secure fair employment opportunities for African Americans. An AFSC worker built connections between African Americans and progressive whites in Little Rock, Arkansas after its school integration crisis in 1957. AFSC work for racial equality in housing, employment, and access to public facilities was important for showing ways that white activists could assist and support the Black civil rights movement as it gathered strength in the 1950s and 1960s.

BOX 6.1   QUAKER CASES AT THE U.S. SUPREME COURT

The responses of individual American Quakers to the American war in Vietnam resulted in two key Supreme Court decisions that expanded the protections for individual belief and advanced the rights of free speech. In 1965, the Court took up the case of Daniel Seeger, a former Catholic who worked for AFSC and claimed conscientious objector status for the military draft even though he did not believe in a supreme being. In *U.S. v. Seeger* (1965), the Court ruled that conscientious objector status could be granted to someone with a consistent set of ethical beliefs parallel to those based on traditional religion. Meanwhile, a handful of Quaker high school students in Iowa wore black armbands to school to protest the war, resulting in their suspension for disruptive behavior. The parents of Mary Beth Tinker (age 13), John Tinker (age 15), and Christopher Eckhardt (age 16) sued the school. The Supreme Court in *Tinker v. Des Moines Community Independent School District* (1969) established that First Amendment rights of political speech extended to public school students, a case that has stood as a strong defense of free speech.

Friends in different countries make different choices for organizing social action. Quaker Peace and Social Witness, successor to the Friends Service Council, functions as a program of Britain Yearly Meeting. Similar groups work in the various European yearly meetings and in Aotearoa/New Zealand, and in Australia through each yearly meeting's Peace and Legislation Committee. Members of AFSC's governing board are Quaker, but it is independent of any yearly meeting. It has grown increasingly professional, employing many non-Quakers with administrative and organizing skills and with personal connections to disadvantaged communities and communities of color. Unlike its early decades when AFSC was oriented to providing opportunities for individual Friends to be of service, it has become a social reform organization oriented to transformative action. The evolution has caused some distress among Friends who no longer see AFSC as their "Quaker" organization, but it also aligns it more closely with the nineteenth century when Quaker ideals and activism leavened wider reform movements.

Friends Committee on National Legislation is the other organization through which Friends in the United States work on a wide variety of peace and social change issues. Rather than working for change at the grassroots, as do many AFSC programs, it seeks to change national policy at the level of the United States Congress. The founding goal of FCNL in 1943 was to push the American government toward disarmament, long-term reduction of military spending, and international reconciliation policies. A founding commitment to peaceful resolution of international conflicts is now coupled with efforts to promote domestic policies around economic justice, human rights, and the needs of Native Americans. Its guiding statement reworks the vision of the Peaceable Kingdom from Isaiah that also inspired Quaker artist Edward Hicks:

> We seek a world free of war and the threat of war.
> We seek a society with equity and justice for all.
> We seek a community where every person's potential may be fulfilled.
> We seek an earth restored.

FCNL is the largest religious lobbying organization in Washington. It develops priorities through extensive consultation with representatives appointed by yearly meetings and coordinates thousands of individual advocates around the country. It works to directly influence lawmaking and executive branch policy implementation. Professional staff based on Capitol Hill lobby directly and support significant citizen lobbying efforts. It strives to develop and maintain a reputation as a nonpartisan advocate and a neutral venue where members of Congress and staff can meet without political posturing, a purpose similar to that of the Quaker United Nations Office.

Lobbying and advocacy from a base of faith avoids the direct necessity to reconcile belief with the compromises of elective office, to which different Friends have responded in different ways.

John Bright served in Parliament from 1843 to 1889, advocating classic liberal ideas of tolerance and economic freedom, but resigned from the cabinet of Prime Minister William Gladstone when the British navy bombarded Alexandria, Egypt. A century later, Philip Noel-Baker served from 1936 to 1970 as a Labour MP and in Labour cabinets, pursuing his political career while helping to form the United Nations and pressing for disarmament. American A. Mitchell Palmer was not so lucky in maintaining his reputation. A progressive Democrat and supporter of Woodrow Wilson, he turned down the offer to be secretary of war because of conflict with his Quaker values, but he is best known for giving voice to American fears of political unrest after World War I, stoking the virulent Red Scare of 1919–20 with what historians call the Palmer Raids on labor leaders and political dissenters. Cape Town Friend H.W. Van Der Merwe facilitated early negotiations which helped end apartheid. Nozizwe Madlala-Routledge, a confirmed pacifist, served as deputy minister of defense in South Africa from 1999 to 2004, challenging the attitude among the military that, "if you want to achieve peace, you must prepare for war." Her service as deputy minister for health ended due to her stance for encouraging treatment of HIV/AIDS. Marian Hobbs, who served in the New Zealand cabinet as minister for the environment and minister for disarmament (1999–2008), summed up the challenge of being a Quaker in politics:

> My parliamentary experience was that awkward and constant compromise of clashing values. There is loyalty to the team and to the overall goal of fairness for all, even when you have doubts about the wisdom, rightness of some of the individual decisions. But to make a fuss, to stand alone, might distract from the main goal.[1]

Concern for the well-being of all people and accompanying efforts to influence public policy toward justice and non-violence is evident in many nations. For instance, in 1961, during the struggle for independence from Britain, Kenyan Friends sent a delegation to meet with Jomo Kenyatta, who was then imprisoned as a leader of the anti-colonial freedom movement. They made this attempt to help break the deadlock between the colonial government and the nationalists even after all the other churches backed out. Kenyatta became the first president of independent Kenya in 1963.

In countries where Quaker presence is extremely small, individual action becomes more visible. In Japan, Inazo Nitobe, who as a young man helped form Japan Yearly Meeting, served in Japan's parliament and as a League of Nations under-secretary-general. Korean Friends included the pacifist and public figure Ham Sok Hon, who was appointed minister of education in his province. He was imprisoned several times for his opposition to both right-wing authoritarian government in South Korea and the North Korean dictatorship.

EQUALITY: ANSWERING THAT OF GOD IN OTHERS

Fit for Freedom, Not for Friendship is a 2009 book co-authored by Donna McDaniel and by Vanessa Julye, an African American Friend who had joined Friends "because I share its belief that there is that of God in everyone." Julye was shocked when she and her family encountered racism within this community despite its historic efforts for abolition of slavery and the participation of many Quakers in the American civil rights movement. The pain of being ignored and unrecognized can be as real in the twenty-first century as it was two centuries earlier when African Americans had to worship on the back benches in the meetinghouse.

The gap between ideals and reality encapsulated by the book's title recognizes both human fallibility and the deep persistence of racial and class prejudice in Western society. Despite the failings she details, the book's final chapter calls for all of us to co-create within the Blessed Community. Hope permeates Julye's ongoing work towards racial justice. She offers suggestions for action including examining individual racial prejudices, learning more about African American history, getting to know individuals of African heritage, and speaking up when offensive statements are made. These are all dimensions of listening beneath the surface and truly seeking out the divine spark in each person we encounter.

BOX 6.2   BAYARD RUSTIN

Bayard Rustin was a powerful figure in the peace and civil rights movements and one of the few prominent African American Friends in the mid-twentieth century. Born in Pennsylvania in 1912, he was raised by his grandmother (a Quaker) and grandfather (a member of the African Methodist Episcopal Church). In his twenties, Rustin joined New York Monthly Meeting and became a committed advocate for racial and social justice, spending time in prison as a conscientious objector during World War II. After the war he worked for the Fellowship of Reconciliation, an interfaith peace and justice organization, and became a close associate of Martin Luther King, Jr. He was the key organizer behind the March on Washington for Jobs and Freedom in 1963, but was forced to remain behind the scenes because of his sexual orientation. He continued to work for peace and civil rights until his death in 1987. He stated repeatedly that Quaker values animated his work. "My activism did not spring from my being gay, or, for that matter, from my being black. Rather, it is rooted fundamentally in my Quaker upbringing and the values that were instilled in me by my grandparents who reared me."

While efforts to achieve racial justice are widespread among Friends, the most visible and explosive work toward full equality within meeting communities in the late twentieth and early twenty-first centuries was around consideration of marriage for gay and lesbian couples and acceptance of individuals of all sexual orientations and gender identities as ministers and leaders. Several yearly meetings and many local meetings have been deeply divided. Some assert a biblical prohibition on same-sex relationships. Others passionately declare that Jesus invites all to hear and respond to the Spirit, just as he listened to and welcomed the woman at the well in John 4, who had many "husbands" and was part of a community rejected by the Hebrews.

STEWARDSHIP: TOWARD A SUSTAINABLE WORLD

Modern Friends add environmental sustainability as an important dimension of simplicity. There is a strong desire to live "in harmony with nature" by reducing one's ecological impact. This may involve simple consumption choices (own only one pair of shoes) or lifestyle choices (no television). It may also slide into something resembling nature worship involving a self-conscious identification with nature as the manifestation as well as the creation of the divine. Simplicity is a way to allow God closer to the individual by paring away unnecessary material trappings, and it is also a way for the individual to come into more direct contact with God as present in the world. At the 2012 World Conference held in Kenya, following a year of worldwide consultation, Friends of all persuasions from around the world accepted what became known as the Kabarak Call to address climate change.

BOX 6.3   THE KABARAK CALL FOR PEACE AND ECOJUSTICE

The Kabarak Call for Peace and Ecojustice was approved on 24 April 2012 at the Sixth World Conference of Friends, held at Kabarak University near Nakuru, Kenya. It is the culmination of the FWCC World Consultation on Global Change which was held in 2010 and 2011.

In past times God's Creation restored itself. Now humanity dominates, our growing population consuming more resources than nature can replace. We must change, we must become careful stewards of all life. Earthcare unites traditional Quaker testimonies: peace, equality, simplicity, love, integrity, and justice. Jesus said, "As you have done unto the least ... you have done unto me."

We are called to work for the peaceable Kingdom of God on the whole earth, in right sharing with all peoples. However few our numbers, we are called to be the salt that flavours and preserves, to be a light in the darkness of greed and destruction.

We have heard of the disappearing snows of Kilimanjaro and glaciers of Bolivia, from which come life-giving waters. We have heard appeals from peoples of the Arctic, Asia and Pacific. We have heard of forests cut down, seasons disrupted, wildlife dying, of land hunger in Africa, of new diseases, droughts, floods, fires, famine and desperate migrations – this climatic chaos is now worsening. There are wars and rumors of war, job loss, inequality and violence. We fear our neighbors. We waste our children's heritage.

All of these are driven by our dominant economic systems – by greed not need, by worship of the market, by Mammon and Caesar.

Is this how Jesus showed us to live?

We are called to see what love can do: to love our neighbor as ourselves, to aid the widow and orphan, to comfort the afflicted and afflict the comfortable, to appeal to consciences and bind the wounds.

We are called to teach our children right relationship, to live in harmony with each other and all living beings in the earth, waters and sky of our Creator, who asks, "Where were you when I laid the foundations of the world?" (Job 38:4)

We are called to do justice to all and walk humbly with our God, to cooperate lovingly with all who share our hopes for the future of the earth.

Twenty-first-century Quakers might be surprised that this insight into the sacred dimension of nature has roots among the earliest Friends. For instance, James Nayler (1715, pp. 260, 261), among the first generation of Quaker leaders, stated in 1656 that "God is in the life of every creature, though few there be that know it." Other seventeenth-century Friends expressed concern for the well-being of animals or became vegetarians, having an awareness of God in all things. While not all modern Friends agree on the existence of a Creator, this thread of concern for the well-being of the earth and its creatures has always been present among Friends. Organizations such as Quaker Ecology Action Network in Canada and the Quaker Earthcare Committee in Australia promote "conscientious protection of our planet" as a parallel to conscientious objection to war.

MISSIONS AS TESTIMONY

Evangelical Friends see mission work as central to fostering the testimonies and goals that unprogrammed Friends address with the SPICES. Mission work has given Quakerism a presence on every continent Establishing missions is concrete evidence of a commitment to make one's life testify to one's faith (see Chapter 3 and Chapter 4). While little known beyond evangelical Friends, mission work has brought Quaker understanding of Christianity to many parts of the world. Ramon González Longoria (in *Being Salt and Light* 2013, p. 65) of Cuba is one of several Friends who spoke to the theme of Salt and Light at the 2012 World Conference of Friends held in Kenya:

> We also need to remember what Matthew 5:16 says: "You should be the light of the world in a way that everyone can see your good work and honour God in heaven." This frees us from the temptation of false pride in our own good works or witness, because the attention should be on God and not on us ... Light reveals things that are all around us, making it possible for us to forget about or not notice the light itself ... As light, we are called to illuminate with our works the darkness of error and injustice.

The intensity of this attention to the Light of Christ that is central to Friends is visible in story after story. Ryna Saynes is a professor at Manila Theological College who worked for years as a paralegal, frequently in jails where she interacted with prisoners who were often confined like sardines in a can. She experienced God's calling to truly see the injustices and horrors in the prison system in the Philippines. Genuine compassion grew in her heart for these "people enveloped in brokenness." She resigned her job but made use of her paralegal training to secure release of nearly 100 prisoners. As this work grew, she worked with women and children and soon created a ministry that was recognized and expanded by the government.

Along with addressing injustice, others brought to Christ by missionary work have felt the same intense, immediate presence of God leading them and protecting them that early Friends did. Karen Patricia Gregorio Henriquez de Calderon from Guatemala described arriving at a hotel just as gunmen shot up the lobby, but she felt God's protection pulling her under a table and saving her life. She sees this experience as an opening to testify and speak for her faith. She spoke at the Sixth World Conference of Friends, which had the theme "Being Salt and Light: Friends living the Kingdom of God in a Broken World." "It has permitted me to demonstrate that God shines in our lives and, with my testimony," she has written. "I can provide flavor to many people who do not have it! This is what it means to live the Kingdom of God in a broken world. Trust thoroughly in His power and strength towards us" (in *Being Salt and Light*, 2013, p. 22).

Evangelicals are conscious of the concerns about cultural imperialism and ways in which Christianity has been embedded and entangled with Western colonialism. Early missions, while concerned with the whole person, had a patronizing dimension, but also a confidence that Africans and others had potential and a desire to gain the tools of Western civilization in the face of colonial power.

By the twenty-first century, much mission work was what might be called "second-wave" – the initiative coming from nations where groups originally converted by Westerners are now moving into new mission fields. For instance, Kenyan Quakers evangelized elsewhere in Africa and occasionally in Latin America, and Central Americans missionaries have worked in the United States. Ron Stansell (2009, pp. 10–11) has drawn on his decades in Bolivia to summarize the perspective of Friends on mission work:

[They] preached salvation by faith, lived out a full consecration to the work of the Holy Spirit in the heart, believed in and promoted social justice and compassion, prayed for physical healing, and exhibited an enthusiasm for the soon return of Christ ... a concept of conversion as a spiritual transformation and a commitment to evangelization as reconciliation and peace with God and neighbor ... They practiced equality and defense of the poor and oppressed in surprising ways ... free of dependency upon the West [and] self-aware as Quakers.

EVERYDAY PROPHETS REVISITED

Early Friends often called one another prophets. Speaking words given by the Spirit and being faithful to the leadings of the Inward Guide are at the core of Quaker practice. In daily attention to this inward guidance Friends may find themselves called to work in prisons or war-torn nations, or as missionaries in foreign lands. William Penn and others described the spiritual task of Friends as "taking up the cross," a daily practice of attention to God and a willingness to let go the demands of the ego. In so doing, they find the impulse to seek wealth, power, or revenge begins to loosen. The dynamic of love is often visible in small, everyday actions as well as in the public arena.

At their best, Friends are a community of everyday prophets who attend to the soul on a daily basis and bring this awareness into their whole community and the larger world around them. In such a community, Friends' manner of worship and ways of doing business teach them much about a new way to live in the world. Other practices, such as offering support and clearness committees, help individuals encourage one another as well as coming to better hear the voice of the Spirit amid the noise of popular culture. Discernment is essential to the grounding of all Quaker action, whether an individual act, a cooperative venture for peace and justice, or a venture into the missionary work. We conclude this chapter by breaking the wall of neutral scholarship with our personal challenge to contemporary Quakers: We are called to be patterns and examples in a twenty-first-century campaigns for peace and ecojustice, as difficult and decisive as the eighteenth- and nineteenth-century drive to abolish slavery. We must all let the living waters flow through us—where we live locally and in wider world fellowship. We must dedicate ourselves to building the peace that passes all understanding, to the repair of the world, opening our lives to the Light to guide us in each small step.

NOTE

1 http://quaker.org.nz/sites/quaker.org.nz/files/Marion%20Hobbs%20QL%202016.pdf

FURTHER READING

Margery Post Abbott, *Everyday Prophets* (Backhouse Lecture, Australia Yearly Meeting, 2016): https://www.quakersaustralia.info/sites/aym-members/ files/pages/files/BL_2016-final-web.pdf (print), https://www.youtube. com/watch?v=99IYoUOhhzw (video). A reminder that Friends can heed the divine call in seemingly ordinary ways.

Donna McDaniel and Vanessa Julye, *Fit for Freedom, Not for Friendship: Quakers, African Americans and the Myth of Racial Justice* (Philadelphia: Friends General Conference, 2009). An account of Quaker interaction with African Americans over three hundred years that challenges contemporary Friends to live up to their ideals.

Parker J. Palmer, *Healing the Heart of Democracy: The Courage to Create Politics Worthy of the Human Spirit* (San Francisco, CA: Jossey-Bass, 2011). A widely read author draws on his Quaker background to argue for a revitalized democracy.

Brian Phillips and John Lampen (Eds.), *Endeavours to Mend: Perspectives on British Quaker Work in the World Today* (London: Quaker Books, 2006).

CONVERGENCE OR PURITY
BEING A QUAKER IN THE
TWENTY-FIRST CENTURY

> [Christ] is 'the real light which enlightens every man' (John 1:9 NEB)
> and makes visible everything that is exposed to the light. And teaches
> all temperance, righteousness, and godliness. And enlightens the
> hearts of all to prepare them for salvation. It is this light which
> reproves the sin of every individual, and if it were not resisted it
> would affect the salvation of all men ... In this light, which Christ
> himself affirms is available to all, communion is enjoyed with the
> Father and with the Son. Wicked men can become holy and lovers of
> that power by whose inward and hidden touches they feel themselves
> turned from evil to good. By it they can learn to treat others as they
> would like to be treated themselves.
>
> (Robert Barclay, *An Apology for the True Christian Divinity*, pp. 72, 73)

As the Religious Society of Friends began to form in the 1600s in
the north of England, increasing numbers caught a similar vision
of Christ leading and teaching them in every aspect of life. They
shared a common culture and language. They challenged the state
church and did not bend in the face of persecution. After nearly
four hundred years Friends live in many nations and speak dozens
of languages. It is no surprise that they have developed different
ways to express their faith. Over the centuries, Friends have
sometimes responded to differences among themselves and from
the surrounding cultures by seeking purity through isolation. At
other times they engaged fully with each other despite their differences, and sought to make the kingdom of God on earth a
reality.

What might the future hold for Quakers? What do Quakers today have to offer the communities in which they live? Their diversity of theology and practice and their global presence make them a microcosm of Christianity. They seek to live in accord with Jesus' teaching even though a significant minority would not identify as Christian. They disagree over questions of purity of belief and practice and face separations over issues of authority.

The excerpt from Barclay's *Apology* that opens this chapter speaks the universalism of early Quakers. They placed faith in the saving grace of Jesus' death, but they did not limit salvation to those who had knowledge of the Bible or the historical Jesus. They knew that grace is available to all people in all times who pay attention to the voice of mercy and justice within their hearts.

In the years since, different strands or "flavors" of Quakers have emphasized different parts of the early message. Most Friends continue to understand the Word of God as the living Christ identified in the opening of the Gospel of John. From this center, some stress the universal dimension of their faith, following the guidance of the Inward Light as they reach across differences within Quakerism or even into Buddhism, Judaism, Islam, and other spiritual traditions. Other Friends have a more orthodox Protestant understanding of the Bible as the Word of God, and some look to the "fundamentals" of Christianity including atonement and the inerrancy of the Bible. As a result, twenty-first-century Friends profess a wide range of perspectives from non-theist to vigorously evangelical. These differing sources of authority may result in divergent Quaker futures that might be summarized as purity and convergence.

DIVERSITY AMONG FRIENDS

As we were writing this chapter, we learned that Congolese immigrants to Canada have organized three evangelical Friends churches among the unprogrammed meetings in Quebec. A younger Quaker from Central American who served as a pastor in southern California took up a ministry in Cambodia. A Kenyan was sent to the Americas to pastor in Belize and help develop the church there. By 2020, three dozen churches in the United States had participated in North American Hispanic Friends Conferences of Spanish-language congregations, some with pastors from Mexico, Guatemala, and other Spanish-speaking nations.

East Africa is the center of gravity in terms of numbers and diversity of Friends. Kenya's twenty-four yearly meetings encompass numerous tribal groups with nearly as many dialects. On the other side of the globe, Evangelical Friends Church Southwest (California, Arizona, and Nevada) has congregations worshipping in English, Spanish, Korean, and Khmer. Some meetings are tiny. Approximately ten people worship at Hill House in Ghana, ten in Cambodia, and 13 in Spain. In contrast, Nepal counts 7,600 Friends. The larger churches are frequently the result of church planting through the efforts of North American based Friends United Meeting or Evangelical Friends Mission. However, more and more church planting efforts are now originating in Africa, Latin America, and Asia independently from the Anglo-centric world.

The majority of individual Friends and Friends churches are in the Global South. Their numbers are growing, especially among disadvantaged people like the Aymara of Bolivia. The furthest northern reach is to Finland Yearly Meeting with 30 members and to the many churches serving native Alaskans in the American state with the highest per capita population of Quakers. The largest concentration of "northern" Friends is the United States and Canada, where the patterns of growth and decline are uneven and most visible at the local meeting level. The decline is greatest in rural areas where outmigration of young people is the norm, and growth more common in urban areas.

The diversity of cultures, languages, and practices are particularly notable given the small total number of Quakers. The evolution of the Society of Friends is now a two-way street. Quakers also offer an ethic that is in at least small ways reshaping local cultures. Friends have brought Alternatives to Violence and other programs for trauma healing and non-violent interactions to every continent. They attract participants to sessions on forgiveness, new ways to interact with neighbors in the aftermath of violence, and tools for aiding in preventing aggression and hostility. At the same time, there are enough Friends in East Africa and in the Andean region of South America to begin reshaping of global Quakerism, at times bringing it closer to the original practice. The Aymara people of

Bolivia, for example, have strong communal values in contrast to the individualism of modern Western cultures. This is reinforced by such practices as in the marriage relationship.

> The old Aymara word for 'to marry' is *jakechana*, which literally means 'to become a person.' ... with both the woman and man equally contributing to the relationship. When a man was appointed to be head of a community ... the appointment actually went to the couple, and the couple would be jointly involved.
>
> (Nancy Thomas, in Abbott and Parsons 2004, p. 178)

Nancy Thomas is one of many Quaker missionaries who set out thinking their role is to teach and found that the real task is to learn. She also states she has learned much about hard work, self-sacrifice, balance, and harmony as well as the ability to see and create beauty in a harsh environment. She names being a listener as the most important of the lessons for cross-cultural ministry along with encouraging the public ministry of local Friends. She encourages nurturing a spirituality of ministry in mission and "listening to God, listening to others, being the persons God wants us to be, and being genuinely present with others—these are the spiritual foundations for the ministry of Public Friends." In saying this, Thomas points to a significant dimension of all Quaker spirituality and practice, namely listening to one another with the sensibility of the Spirit.

WHO SPEAKS FOR FRIENDS?

The intellectual center of Friends is still the English-speaking world if for no other reason than the ease of communication. British Friends maintain a special place within the Religious Society of Friends largely because of their role in nurturing the formation of this movement. Many of the founding stories are based in the British Isles. *Faith and Practice* of Britain Yearly Meeting is often consulted, especially as yearly meetings are drafting their own volumes.

Friends like to write about their lives and their faith. *Quaker Life, Friends Journal, Friends Quarterly, Western Friend, Canadian Friend*, and *The Australian Friend* are news and opinion publications.

Quaker Theology, Quaker Studies, and *Quaker Religious Thought* are leading outlets for Quaker scholarship. Britain Yearly Meeting publishes its annual Swarthmore Lecture and Australia Yearly Meeting publishes its annual Backhouse Lecture. The Pendle Hill Quaker study center outside Philadelphia has continued the early Friends habit of pamphleteering by issuing over 500 "Pendle Hill Pamphlets" since 1934; many of them have been highly influential in furthering the spiritual life of unprogrammed Friends. This long-established bent, combined with centuries of detailed record keeping, means that Friends have created a hefty archive of journals, pamphlets, treatises, and documentation that makes them a prime subject for historians and literature specialists, resulting in a body of scholarship out of proportion to their numbers.

A number of Quaker thinkers are widely read and influential beyond the Society of Friends. In the mid-twentieth century, the devotional writings of Rufus Jones and Thomas Kelly opened doorways into the individual experience of the divine. In recent decades, evangelical pastor and seminary professor Richard Foster has promoted ecumenical Christian renewal through the Renovaré movement and books like *A Celebration of Discipline* (1980). Parker J. Palmer has written extensively about the importance for educators and political activists to draw on deep spiritual grounding as the foundation for their work in books like *Let This Life Speak* (1997) and *Healing the Heart of Democracy* (2011).

Kenyan publishers are now issuing contemporary English-language writing by East African Friends. Britain Yearly Meeting in 2016 invited Esther Mombo and Cécile Nyiramana to give its annual lecture, which has been published and widely distributed. British and American editors and writers are becoming aware of the importance of including voices from around the globe. Increasingly North American Spanish speakers are translating writings of Fox, Barclay, and other prominent Friends into Spanish as Latin Americans seek to better understand the theological underpinnings of various Quaker practices, especially in regard to the outward sacraments.

Friends from the more oral cultures of the Southern Hemisphere are finding opportunities and encouragement to articulate their experience on paper for wider communication. Major Quaker organizations are more systematically attempting to insure that plenary speakers and workshop leaders at international conferences reflect the demographics of Friends. As Andean and other Latino Friends claim their rightful voice, will it be in Spanish, or in Aymara? Similar questions can be asked about French speaking Friends in the Great Lakes district of Africa. Will Kenyans prefer Swahili or the western Kenyan languages to English? What efforts will be made to translate such works into English? Will the center of gravity for writing about Friends come to match the demographic center, and will North American and British Friends be invigorated by these new articulations? Certainly many such Friends have found the personal interactions around the world to be enriching and enlivening.

SOURCES OF DISCORD

In 2015 Northwest Yearly Meeting in the United States "released" one of its churches from the larger body. The Board of Elders wrote a letter to West Hills Friends Church, which had publicly welcomed people with a range of sexualities, stating that the yearly meeting could not tolerate the full range of beliefs. The Elders asserted that West Hills would be more likely to thrive if removed from the larger body. It was the third such separation in a decade, following similar splits in Indiana and North Carolina. Disagreement about welcoming non-heterosexuals into membership and publicly recognizing their marriages or their ministries were the triggering issues in each case, and have been points of disagreement in other yearly meetings. Underpinning the discussions have been unspoken matters of authority: Who gets to interpret the Bible? Who has the final say in decision-making?

People have strikingly different responses to issues of authority. Some value the security of a firm leader and a clear set of guidelines; others chafe at any restriction on their behaviors as individuals. The same is true of institutions and of churches. Catholics find the leadership of the Pope and the formal teachings of the church to be central in understanding their faith. Many Protestants view the Bible as the central source of authority. Friends offer yet another way: looking to the Light of Christ as Word of God and Inward Guide which for many is the primary authority for their lives. None of these differing approaches has prevented separations in the Christian church over the centuries—nor have Quakers been immune to the tension between organization and individualism since the days of George Fox and James Nayler.

Friends have a relatively flat hierarchy and no body speaks definitively for Quakers worldwide. However, there are variations in how Friends treat their books of *Faith and Practice*. Some are purely descriptive of current practice and others are proscriptive for members of yearly meetings. As a consequence some of these yearly meetings are strongly congregational and others give more authority to the central leadership. Many of the more recent separations have been over matters of authority, particularly who gets to interpret Bible passages. There are also instances of individuals claiming authority over behavior or control of funds. Kenyan Friend Zablon Malenge in "Early Christianity Revived in the Perspective of Friends in Kenya" (2012, p. 88) describes it this way:

> [L]eadership in some of our Quaker meetings seems to be regarded as a source of power rather than service. Here, it is difficult to distinguish between authority and power because authority is usually equated with power ... hence the mushrooming and proliferation of splinter groups, factions, ministries and churches. It is either way. These factions are either running away from authoritarian leadership or are desirous of being in a similar position where they also can exercise their authority.

The 2015 separation in Northwest Yearly Meeting happened when a central committee decided that any local meeting that did not accept its rejection of homosexuality was no longer a member of the community. In response, seven monthly meetings established a new regional body, Sierra-Cascades Yearly Meeting, which defines itself as a "voluntary association of meetings, churches, and individuals that supports worship, ministry, and service through the cultivation of Christian faith in the Quaker tradition." The new yearly meeting has committed itself to recognizing the full participation of all individuals in all of aspects of its life independent of their sexual orientation or gender identity.

The trigger for the schism in Indiana Yearly Meeting was also the decision by one of its prominent meetings to adopt a statement welcoming all individuals into full participation, with several other churches in sympathy. The yearly meeting wrestled with the resulting disagreement for several years before undertaking a process of "reconfiguration" that led to a proposal to divide the yearly meeting and its assets. Fifteen monthly meetings, quite diverse in character and theology, chose to leave and form the New Association of Friends with no decision-making authority over member churches. What they shared was a conviction that they wanted to be part of a more decentralized authority. Some in the New Association felt pushed out; others felt relief.

On the traditionally Christian side of a theological spectrum, the attractions of charismatic evangelical worship are a challenge to Quakers in the Global South. Africa and Latin America Friends churches have resisted the use of Pentecostal practices such as speaking in tongues as other than a private devotional practice, contrary to the fast growth of Pentecostalism in Africa and Latin America. This places them at odds with other evangelicals around them. At times this has set off a generational struggle around the desire of younger Friends for louder music and more energy in their worship services. In Kenya, Kifa Ayuba helped found the Avakambuli (African Holy Spirit) church in 1927, which has grown to several hundred thousand members. In the US, a similar disagreement resulted in John Wimber and other evangelicals in the 1980s forming the Vineyard Church, which has become a worldwide movement with more than 2,000 churches.

The more theologically liberal meetings have avoided dramatic divisions in the twentieth and twenty-first centuries, despite the substantial range of theology often be present within any given community. Individual Friends in unprogrammed meetings may be devoutly Christian or passionately non-theist, to name the extremes, but as long as they are willing to take care with the language they use, most are willing to hold these differences in tension. They may disagree over appropriate behavior or ministries, but more often those who are most uncomfortable quietly (or not so quietly) pack up and leave the community. The leakage happens on both sides. Christian Friends find vocal "peace and sunshine" ministries in meeting for worship unnourishing and get tired of complaints when they cite the Bible. Other Friends who are refugees from rigid Christian upbringings find that the same Christian ministries bring up painful memories that push them away.

Conflicts and disagreements characterize human relationships. Some respond by refusing to openly admit to anger or other painful dimensions of their interactions. Quakers have an unusual challenge, given that most point to the Light of Christ or the Spirit as the ultimate authority, rather than to the Bible or to designated individuals with the power to declare a decision in the face of substantial objections. One can say that what makes a church or meeting "Quaker" is making decisions in a meeting for worship where everyone listens and trusts in the guidance of the spirit. In seeking the sense of the meeting, Friends are not demanding unanimity, but an awareness that a particular action is for the benefit of the community and in accord with the Inward Teacher and with Jesus' teachings. When people take unilateral action, they break that trust and separations often have been the most obvious way forward. Such are a few of the factors that set the conditions for the twenty-first century and the contrasting pulls towards purity and towards convergence.

PURITY AND UNITY

Purity can take many forms. For George Fox it was a spiritual state resulting from connection with the divine. He drew on the imagery of Genesis 3:24 to describe the experience of purity when, unlike Adam and Eve expelled from Eden, he "was come up in spirit through the flaming sword into the paradise of God … [when] all the creation gave another smell unto me than before." Purity can also mean adherence to specific standard beliefs and practices. The desire for different types of purity has fueled many divisions over the centuries, even as it has played a role in the survival of Friends as a religious movement and a people conscious of the distinction between secular culture and the demands of faith. In the twenty-first century, the impulse to purity can interfere with peace and justice work when Christian Friends refuse to work with anyone who does not profess Jesus as Savior, while liberal Friends may be equally uncomfortable working with those who emphasize the Bible and personal salvation.

A more positive dimension of purity is the rejection of those aspects of secular culture that encourage people to amass wealth or to focus their lives on gaining power over others. Friends profess a standard of truth-telling that sets them apart from the culture of lies which seem so prevalent. They carry a vision a world without war that permeates their efforts to seek the causes of violence rather than simply returning violence for violence. They refuse to follow cultural norms without critical examination and discernment of whether their words and actions are in accord with creating God's kingdom. In so doing they have set a standard for themselves that is not always met, but at least prompts them to reflect on their decisions in a deliberate way.

The process of discernment is central to Friends. To ask themselves each day, "Is this task, are these words, in accord with that still, small voice within that marks the guidance of the Holy Spirit?" Accountability to the Spirit, to the Light of Christ, runs counter to the individualism of western culture and to the animism of other cultures where Quakerism has taken hold. In making corporate decisions, Friends seek unity or the sense of the meeting. British Friends express it this way in their *Faith and Practice* (1994, p. 17): "Friends find unity in the depth of silence … We struggle with differences in our meetings for church affairs and here too, we know the experience of unity in conviction and purpose. It is a unity … in discovering the place in which we can stand together."

Such decision-making holds promise of a revised approach for dealing with the problems that result from the changing climate. The threat of rising sea levels has already begun to displace low-lying communities and it is all too easy for those with money and power to dictate the actions to be taken without regard for the rights of those most vulnerable. This small group of people who are Friends cannot and should not make major decisions for others, but perhaps they hold some value for the world in the questions they ask and the respect for others that arises from their belief that there is that of God in every heart.

COMMUNICATION AND CONVERGENCE

At the World Conference of Friends in 1991 Kenyan men were very much at odds with one another over a variety of issues, but the women decided this was not acceptable and not part of their faith. Kenyan women from every yearly meeting made the commitment to join together in prayer. This practice continued upon their return home and became foundational to the United Society of Friends Women in Kenya, building connections across the nation. A decade or so later, several individuals at a gathering of North American Quaker leaders spontaneously stood and approached those who belonged to churches on the opposite sides of past, painful divisions. Their purpose was to confess to damaging actions of their predecessors and to ask forgiveness of those who were harmed.

The Society of Friends has no central authority over its dozens of independent yearly meetings—no doctrinal and administrative hierarchy like Roman Catholicism or single policy-making body like the General Conference of the United Methodist Church. At the same time, Friends have always been indefatigable communicators across distance and theological divisions, penning pamphlets, supporting traveling ministers, and repeatedly convening to talk through differences. The primary worldwide Quaker organization, the Friends World Committee for Consultation (FWCC), emerged from a succession of such meetings in the 1920s and 1930s among younger British and American Friends impatient with old divisions. In 1937, participants in a "world conference" in Philadelphia organized FWCC to encourage communication across long-standing differences. Its purposes, as stated in 1952, are "to encourage and strengthen the spiritual life within the Society," to promote an understanding of "the worldwide character of the Society," to support consultation across cultures, countries, and languages, and to facilitate the presentation of Quaker views on world affairs.

FWCC is an important connector for Quakers worldwide. It has a small central office in London and "sections" for the Americas, Europe and the Middle East, Africa, and Asia-Pacific, each with its own minuscule staff. FWCC provides a membership home for Friends who are isolated from established meetings. It sponsors traveling ministers and visitation among English-speaking and Spanish-speaking Quakers in the Americas, among European and African Quakers, and among Asian, Australian, and New Zealand Friends. Its most substantial and far-reaching work has been periodic international gatherings of Quakers from all regions and faith traditions. Early meetings took place at familiar sites in Britain and the United States, but in 1991 FWCC recognized Quaker diversity by holding the Fifth World Conference of Friends in three venues: Kenya, Honduras, and the Netherlands. The Sixth World Conference in 2012 was in Kenya. Since then FWCC has also organized other large international gatherings in New Zealand in 2007 and Peru in 2016, with South Africa on the docket for 2023.

The other role of FWCC is to represent Quakers in international bodies. It is an associate member of the World Council of Churches, allowing its executive secretary the occasional opportunity to rub elbows with dignitaries and leaders of vastly larger Christian churches. The United Nations approved consultative status for FWCC in 1948, and Friends established the Quaker United Nations Office (QUNO). FWCC provides the umbrella for QUNO, whose New York office is jointly administered with the American Friends Service Committee. Its Geneva office cooperates with Britain Yearly Meeting's Quaker Peace and Social Witness. The UN granted QUNO "general status" on 2002, allowing staff to participate more fully in committee meetings and to suggest agenda items for the UN Economic and Social Council.

In the United States, one of FWCC's early accomplishments was to help convene a conference in St. Louis in 1970 that addressed the question, "What future for Friends?" Much energy for the meeting came from leading evangelical Quaker Everett Cattell, who persuaded Friends United Meeting and Evangelical Friends Alliance to invite unprogrammed Quakers to join in finding common ground. The first such gathering of all American Quakers since the 1920s, it generated both enthusiasm and discomfort with Quaker ecumenism and produced an important collection of essays—*What Future for Friends?*—that foreshadowed the "convergent Friends" movement of the twenty-first century.

While FWCC operates with the standard forms of committees and face-to-face conferences, the convergent Friends take their cue from the possibilities of electronic community. Coined by Robin Mohr in 2006, the term "convergent Friends" refers to new efforts to share spiritual journeys and insights across the different Quaker flavors in the United States and Canada. Convergent Friends are a loose movement rather than an organization, connected by personal relations, blogs, and websites such as QuakerQuaker.org that aggregate Quaker thinking and commentary from multiple perspectives. The implicit goal is dialogue and joint worship rather than agreement; participants distinguish convergence or coming together from consolidation or unification, and some parse the term as combining the "conservative" reinvigoration of traditional Quakerism combined with the "emergence" of new forms of expression and communication. Participants tend to come from the politically liberal side of evangelical Friends and from more Christian Friends among unprogrammed meetings.

An example of convergence on the ground rather than among the electrons is the Pacific Northwest Quaker Women's Theology Conference. Held biennially since 1995, it grew out of informal meetings among women from Northwest Yearly Meeting (evangelical) and North Pacific Yearly Meeting (unprogrammed) who set aside doctrinal differences in favor of worshipful engagement and relationship building. Such connections help to break down fears and misconceptions in their churches about lesbians and gays while emphasizing the centrality of discernment of the Holy Spirit in decision-making and giving support to liberal women who wished to speak about Jesus. Participants largely ignore institutional affiliations and understand "doing theology" as sharing stories of individual faith journeys, updating the long tradition of Quakers publishing their spiritual journals and testimonies of faith. During the business meeting at the end of each conference the question is raised if they should meet again, which only happens if enough women step forward at that moment to take on the organization.

CONCLUSIONS

A central question for twenty-first century Friends is the strength of their distinctive practices for decision-making and their testimony to peace and non-violence. Can they can find ways to demonstrate to the world that it is possible to act together to lift up just solutions to difficult problems and solve serious disagreements without resorting to violence and rigid authoritarian governance?

In this time of intolerance and separation among Friends the question arises whether decision-making is truly grounded in the Spirit. To what degree have Friends been unwilling to wait in the Light together long enough to find unity rather than responding to the divisive pressures of secular society?

Over the centuries, Friends have varied in their level of interactions with the world around them. The earliest years were a time of engagement filled with conviction that they had been shown a way to bring about God's kingdom on earth for all people everywhere. Following the decades of persecution, Friends entered into a period of Quietism when they largely lived in small communities of other Friends, shared in business dealings, and otherwise kept apart from the secular culture. As they emerged from this self-imposed isolation, differences that had remained in the background became more visible, particularly as the commitment to end slavery grew and choices arose between remaining a people apart and creating coalitions with like-minded non-Friends.

Simultaneously, Friends became more a part of the culture around them. Some chose a more orthodox Protestant approach and others were drawn towards modernism and questioning of the Bible. As the more evangelical of Friends scattered around the world, reviving the missionary zeal of early Quakers, they encountered cultures that did not always share Anglo-American values. But the pressures to divide were matched by the desire of many Friends to heal the divisions. Several yearly meetings in the United States reunited in the mid-twentieth century. A number of these reunited meetings became predominantly liberal in their theology and politics, but they also retained membership in the centrist body, Friends United Meeting, which has worked to hold together the sometimes contradictory stances of its constituent yearly meetings in both the United States and East Africa.

Contemporary liberal and academic Friends have looked at Western demographics and projected the demise of Quakerism. Certainly, this group was small to begin with and has repeatedly splintered. Many meetings and churches in native English-speaking nations comment on the high percentage of older people at worship and the scarcity of children and young adults. People in other parts of the globe have been more enthusiastic about the good news brought by missionaries, whose work has been rewarded with growth and the development of local institutions. Converts have taken advantage of educational opportunities and a discipline that provides the basis for successful careers. They have also shown great courage in the face of genocide in Rwanda and Burundi and ongoing harassment and violence in Palestine, East Africa, or parts of Latin America.

Some Quakers focus on the need for correct Christian belief. Others reject specific doctrines about Christ, but still follow a way of life that can be readily found in the Christian Testament. Friends of all flavors assert that a peaceful world depends on learning ways to listen for the divine Guide as well as responding respectfully to those who disagree with them. Diversity itself can be a blockage, a challenge, or an opportunity, depending on how Friends respond. At their best, Friends seek ways to worship together as well as to work together to live out a vision of God's kingdom. They look to a world where all speak with integrity, settle differences non-violently, live with a spirit of generosity, eschewing greed, building a community based on respect and just treatment of all, and caring for the whole of this planet that sustains us.

FURTHER READING

Angelina Conti, Cara Curtis, C. Wess Daniels, et al. (Eds.), *Spirit Rising: Young Quaker Voices* (Philadelphia: Quaker Press of Friends General Conference, 2010). An anthology of short essays and reflections by more than one hundred fifty younger Friends from around the world.

C. Wess Daniels and Rhiannon Grant (Eds.), *The Quaker World* (Routledge, forthcoming 2021). Essays that describe and represent the worldwide reach of twenty-first-century Quakerism.

APPENDIX: QUAKERS IN FICTION

Quakers make frequent appearances in fiction for such a small denomination. A bibliography compiled by Anna Breiner Caulfield in 1993 identified more than 600 titles. Although Quakers are sometimes the central character, authors often use them to provide a contrast to more conventional characters, either as to model virtue or to suggest that devotion to high ideals is impractical. A very early example of the first is by the famous Daniel Defoe. His *The Life, Adventures and Piracies of the Famous Captain Singleton* (1720) includes a Quaker doctor who becomes the conscience of a pirate ship after his capture. The second storyline is central to the classic western film *High Noon* (1952) in which the Quaker bride (Grace Kelly) of a former sheriff (Gary Cooper) realizes at the end that it is necessary to use force to resist the murderous bad guys. Quakers also make a surprising number of appearances in science fiction, which traditionally emphasizes fast action and strong individual characters. Quakers as individuals or more often as communities provide the opportunity for authors to explore and test alternatives to the colonial or imperial assumptions of space exploration fiction.

This list includes several novels that introduce the Quaker experience and values to children, young adults, and adult readers.

HISTORICAL FICTION

Tracy Chevalier, *The Last Runaway* (2013). English Quaker Honor Bright travels to America, finds support among Friends, and becomes involved with the Underground Railroad.

Marguerite de Angeli, *Thee, Hannah* (1940). Nine-year old Hannah chafes against her Philadelphia Quaker upbringing but learns to appreciate simplicity in a classic children's book.

Henry Grifford, *The Lost Years* (1987). A Quaker ironmonger in eighteenth-century England.

Jan de Hartog, *The Peaceable Kingdom* (1971) and *The Peculiar People* (1992). In the first book, de Hartog explores the founding of Quakerism by George Fox and Margaret Fell and Quaker struggles with slavery in the New World. The second is set in Indiana during the Hicksite separation of the early nineteenth century.

Sue Monk Kidd, *The Invention of Wings* (2014). The fictionalized lives of Sarah and Angelina Grimké, radical abolitionists and feminists who joined with the Society of Friends and then left because they were too radical for conservative Quakers.

Barbara Schell Luetke, *The Kendall Sparrow: A Novel of Elizabeth Fletcher* (2019). A fictionalized life of a young woman who was one of the Valiant Sixty.

James Michener, *Chesapeake* (1978). A saga that follows several families through multiple generations. The Quaker Paxmores experience imprisonment and persecution in England and the dilemmas of slavery and warfare in the United States.

Sally Nichols, *Things a Bright Girl Can Do* (2017). A young adult novel about three girls, one of them a Quaker, in London during World War I.

Rose Tremain, *Restoration: A Novel of the Seventeenth Century* (1989). A physician to King Charles II abandons a life of luxury to help Quakers run a hospital for the mentally ill in this highly regarded novel. The film adaptation in 1995 has an all-star cast of Robert Downey, Jr., Ian McKellen, Meg Ryan, and Hugh Grant, but was not a box-office success.

Brinton Turkel, *Obadiah the Bold* (1965). The first of four short illustrated children's books about a Quaker boy growing up on Nantucket during the whaling era who learns Friendly lessons in honesty and friendship.

Ann Turnbull, *No Shame, No Fear* (2004). In 1662 England, Susanna and Will reenact the Romeo and Juliet story as Quaker girl loves wealthy Puritan boy in the face of religious conflict and persecution.

Jessamyn West, *The Friendly Persuasion* (1945). Linked stories depict a loving Quaker family in Indiana facing moral choices during the American Civil War; it was the basis of a popular movie in 1956.

SCIENCE FICTION

Molly Gloss, *The Dazzle of Day* (1997). When a huge self-contained starship carrying thousands of Quakers reaches its destination after several generations, the voyagers must decide whether to settle on a very inhospitable planet or continue into the unknown. Gloss offers a remarkably sensitive depiction of the Quaker business process through which they make their decision.

Nancy Kress, *Crossfire* (2003). "New Quakers" are one of several groups colonizing a planet who find themselves caught in an interstellar war between two other space-faring species. Sitting in silence and waiting for the Light has some positive results but falls short as a full solution for galactic conflict.

Judith Moffett, *Pennterra* (1987). Two human colonies on the planet that the first Quaker colonists have named Pennterra take different approaches in their interactions with the native hrossa, discovering that it is necessary to adapt to both the planet itself and to the power of the hrossa.

David Morse, *The Iron Bridge* (1998). A young woman from eco-logically devastated 2043 travels back in time to England in the 1770s in an attempt to sabotage the plans for the iron bridge that Quaker Abraham Darby is building over the River Severn. She hopes that collapse of the bridge will set back the Industrial Revolution and mitigate its destructive environmental impacts.

Joan Slonczewski, *Still Forms on Foxfield* (1980). A Quaker settlement on the planet Foxfield has developed a modus vivendi with the native people over the course of a century. When the United Nations Interplanetary arrives, tension builds between the newcomers and the long-isolated Quakers and with the native inhabitants who threaten to destroy the UNI.

Joan Slonczewski, *The Wall around Eden* (1989). In the aftermath of nuclear war, aliens have saved the remaining humans by enclosing communities inside protective walls. A young woman rebels against the passivity of the largely Quaker enclave Glynwood (in Pennsylvania) and finds her way through the barrier to learn what lies behind the actions of the aliens.

GLOSSARY

Quakers use a number of common words in distinctive ways that are often puzzling to outsiders.

business
meeting

Friends conduct the business of the community as a meeting for worship with attention to business. All members, and in many meetings attenders as well, are encouraged to participate in the monthly meetings for business where all major decisions are made. The intent of Friends business meetings is to determine where the Spirit is leading the group in this time and place.

centering

The process of opening one's heart and mind to the workings of the Light, usually within the context of worship.

church

Friends believe that the people are the church, not the building, thus many Friends speak of their worship space as the meetinghouse. Evangelical Friends often speak of themselves as the Friends Church.

clearness

The process of seeking discernment about individual decisions with support of a group. Meetings may also appoint clearness committees regarding proposed membership, marriage or other decisions which require community agreement as well as individual clearness.

clerk

The clerk of a meeting is the individual who presides at business meeting and may represent a

	meeting publicly. The task of the clerk is to lay out the agenda, to listen for the sense of the meeting, then to name the decision that the community has come to. An individual may also clerk a committee, or be clerk of the governing board of a large organization.
concern	A concern is an issue on which an individual experiences a strong spiritual calling for action. A concern may involve work within the Society of Friends or in the world at large.
Conservative Friends	A small group of Quakers who practice unprogrammed worship with a strong Christian orientation and emphasize simplicity. They see themselves as continuing the essence of early Quakerism.
convincement/ conviction	Convincement is the process through which individuals decide to accept Quaker beliefs and practices. Liberal Quakers like the term because it implies a thoughtful intellectual choice. Evangelical Quakers see it as another way to describe conversion to a Christian faith. It derives from the early Quaker use of "conviction" for the process by which the Inner Light revealed a person's sins, of which he was "convicted" in his own mind, but with the Light then showing a path the forgiveness and redemption.
elder	An elder is a person of any age with recognized abilities to nurture the growth of the spirit in others by encouraging spiritual gifts and suggesting behaviors that might help someone to be a more effective participant in worship. In earlier centuries Quakers sometimes emphasized the disciplinary function of "eldering."
epistle	Yearly meetings, and at times other Quaker bodies, write epistles addressed to "all Friends everywhere" reporting on their annual sessions and noting how God is at work among them. Historically, individual Friends, such as George Fox, would write epistles following the example of Paul and others in the Christian Testament.

evangelical friends | A term used to refer to Friends who belong to yearly meetings that profess belief in Jesus Christ and where Friends largely worship in programmed meetings. Often such Friends call themselves part of the Friends Church rather than the Religious Society of Friends.

Faith and Practice/Book of Discipline | Volumes published by yearly meetings that include statements about Quaker beliefs and outline procedures for the everyday operations of local meetings ("discipline" referring to a set of rules). In evangelical meetings the statements about belief tend to be prescriptive, whereas liberal meetings may choose to make more open-ended statements and include a range of relevant quotations from Quakers over the centuries.

First Day/ First Month | Early Friends objected to the use of pagan names for the days and months and spoke only of "first day" instead of Sunday and "first month" instead of January, and so through seventh day and twelfth month.

Hicksites | North American Quakers in several East Coast yearly meetings separated in 1827 creating new bodies known as Hicksites (often more rural) and Orthodox Friends (often urban based). Hicksites saw Orthodox Friends as emphasizing the authority of the Bible at the expense of direct religious experience. Hicksites are often seen as one of the roots from which modern liberal Quakerism developed.

leading | A movement of the Spirit guiding an individual to particular words or actions. A person may be led to speak during unprogrammed worship, led to travel in the ministry, or led to act on a concern, such as care for the homeless or witness against war.

liberal Friends | A term used to refer to Friends who are open to a range of theological belief and who are generally liberal on political and social issues. Most liberal Friends worship in unprogrammed meetings.

Light/Inward   Friends initially called themselves "Children of the
Light/Inner   Light" referring to the Light of Christ which they
Light   believe is available to every person (see the first
               chapter of the Gospel of John), whether they know
               of Jesus or not. The Light is both a guide and a
               monitor. Its transforming work is central.

meeting   The word "meeting" is used to refer to the time of
               worship on First Day mornings and also as the
               name for the community which worships together
               (e.g., Langley Hill Friends Meeting).

minutes   The records of decisions by a local or yearly meet-
               ing. Some minutes relate to everyday meeting
               operations. Others are intended as public statements
               on religious, social and political issues.

meetinghouse   The building where Friends worship is known as
               the meetinghouse and may be a home, an old fac-
               tory building, or a specially built structure, but is
               not held to be a consecrated space. Groups of
               Friends will worship in any space available.

monthly   The basic worshipping community of Friends and
meeting/village the body in which membership is held. Members
meeting   of a monthly meeting meet weekly or more often
               for worship and monthly to conduct the business of
               the meeting. East African Friends usually speak of
               village meetings rather than monthly meetings.

non-pastoral/ A religious group such as a Friends Meeting that
pastoral   operates without a single designated leader who is
               paid to preach and look after the congregation is
               "non-pastoral," as opposed to a pastoral church
               with a lead pastor/minister/priest and often other
               staff. Early Friends were fierce opponents of the
               pastoral system and its "hireling ministers."

opening/   An opening is an insight or personal transformation
continuing   that "opens" new spiritual understanding. It is a
revelation   contemporary way to talk about the doctrine of
               continuing revelation, by which early Quakers
               meant that God remained active and accessible at
               all times to those who opened themselves to the
               workings of the divine.

Orthodox Friends
: The American Quakers who valued the Bible over the Inward Light as guidance and separated from Hicksites in the eastern United States beginning in 1828. Several Hicksite and Orthodox yearly meetings rejoined in the 1950s.

programmed/ semi-programmed
: The majority of Friends worldwide worship in a form similar to Protestant church services with hymn singing, Bible readings, and a planned message (sermon) offered by the pastor. Since many of these churches, particularly in the United States, hand out printed programs, the term "programmed" has become attached to this form of worship. Quaker pastors, however, will at times find they have no message to give and offer a longer period of "open" or "unprogrammed" worship where anyone may speak out of the silence as lead. Semi-programmed meetings may simply include a short Bible reading, a hymn or two and perhaps someone in the congregation to offer a five-minute message, leaving the bulk of the hour in open, expectant worship.

quarterly meeting/area meeting
: The quarterly meeting in the United States and the area meeting in Britain are regional groupings of local meetings that nest organizationally within yearly meetings. Area meetings have substantially more authority and functions than do American quarterly meetings.

queries
: Sets of questions that ask Friends to reflect on their faith and how it translates into action. In books of Faith and Practice they are sometimes paired with Advices, which are suggestions for right action.

released Friend
: Early Quakers would "release" members from financial and community obligations for a period of time so that they could travel in the ministry. In nineteenth-century America, they began to release individuals for the specific purpose of pastoring a church, starting the evolution toward employing full-time clergy. Contemporary liberal Quakers use

the term the recognize someone called to special work who needs relief from meeting obligations and perhaps financial support.

sacraments
Friends believe that the sacraments are an inward and spiritual experience. While the outward sacraments such as baptism and communion are not wrong, Friends have always held that the focus on the external bread and wine or water can get in the way of knowing the direct baptism of the Holy Spirit and the communion which is at the heart of every gathered meeting for worship.

sense of the meeting
Quakers seek to come to common understanding in decision making. They come to the "sense of the meeting" when the group shares broad agreement, although not necessarily unanimity. It can emerge both incrementally and unexpectedly.

testimonies
How to live in the world is central to Friends' faith, and often Friends will use the term "testimonies" to refer to how their lives witness the Light and Truth. In the late twentieth century, many Friends began to name the central testimonies as simplicity, peace, integrity, community, equality, and stewardship (SPICES), concepts which underlie all dimensions of life. Evangelical Friends often speak of offering their testimony to the work of Christ in the heart. These eternal truths often are expressed in the form of distinctive behaviors that vary over time and culture.

unprogrammed worship
Friends' belief that God is available to all people without the need of a priest, or even the Bible, to mediate has given rise to their unusual form of worship where individuals gather in expectant silence. In the silence, Friends listen for the movement of the Spirit and, at times, an individual will feel words rising which he or she is led to offer to the gathered group as vocal ministry. A gathered or covered meeting is a time when many present are aware of the divine presence among them and a sense of communion. This may occur even if no words are spoken.

yearly
meeting
All the monthly meetings and worship groups in a region jointly form the yearly meeting, although there may be two or more such bodies with differing theology and practice in any given region. This body normally holds an annual meeting where Friends gather to worship together and conduct business of mutual interest. The yearly meeting has responsibility for creating the book of Faith and Practice used in that region.

BIBLIOGRAPHY

OVERVIEWS

Stephen W. Angell and Pink Dandelion, *The Cambridge Companion to Quakerism* (Cambridge, UK: Cambridge University Press, 2018).

Stephen W. Angell and Pink Dandelion, *The Oxford Handbook of Quaker Studies* (Oxford, UK: Oxford University Press, 2018).

Howard Brinton and Margaret Hope Bacon, *Friends for 350 Years* (Wallingford, PA: Pendle Hill Publications, 2002).

Wilmer Cooper, *A Living Faith: A Historical Study of Quaker Beliefs* (Richmond, IN: Friends United Press, 1990).

Pink Dandelion, *An Introduction to Quakerism* (Cambridge, UK: Cambridge University Press, 2007).

Pink Dandelion, *The Quakers: A Very Short Introduction* (New York: Oxford University Press, 2008).

J. William Frost and Hugh Barbour, *The Quakers* (Westport, CT: Greenwood, 1988).

Thomas Hamm, *The Quakers in America* (New York: Columbia University Press, 2003).

Daisy Newman, *A Procession of Friends* (Richmond, IN: Friends United Press, 1972),

John Punshon, *Portrait in Grey* (London: Quaker Home Service, 1984).

D. Elton Trueblood, *The People Called Quakers* (New York: Harper & Row, 1966).

Walter R. Williams, *The Rich Heritage of Quakerism* (Newberg, OR: Barclay Press, 1962/1987).

REFERENCES AND ANTHOLOGIES OF QUAKER WRITING

Margery Post Abbott, *A Certain Kind of Perfection: An Anthology of Evangelical and Liberal Quaker Writers* (Wallingford, PA: Pendle Hill Publications, 1997).

Margery Post Abbott, Mart Ellen Chijioke, Pink Dandelion, and John Oliver, Jr., *Historical Dictionary of the Friends (Quakers)* (Lanham, MD: Scarecrow Press, 2012).

Mary Garman, Judith Applegate, Margaret Benefiel, and Dortha Meredith, *Hidden in Plain Sight: Quaker Women's Writing, 1650–1700* (Wallingford, PA: Pendle Hill Publications, 1996).

Thomas Hamm, *Quaker Writings: An Anthology, 1650–1920* (New York: Penguin, 2010).

Douglas Steere, *Quaker Spirituality: Selected Works* (New York: Paulist Press: 1984).

Jessamyn West, *A Quaker Reader* (Wallingford, PA: Pendle Hill Publications, 1962/1992).

QUAKER CLASSICS

Robert Barclay, *Barclay's Apology in Modern English*, ed. Dean Freiday (Manasquam, NJ, 1967).

Margaret Fell, *Undaunted Zeal: The Letters of Margaret Fell*, ed. Elsa F. Glines (Richmond, IN: Friends United Press, 2003).

George Fox, *The Journal of George Fox*, ed. J.L. Nickalls (Cambridge UK: Cambridge University Press, 1952).

Rufus Jones, *Rufus Jones: Essential Writings*, ed. Kerry Walters (Maryknoll, NY: Orbis, 2001).

Thomas Kelly, *A Testament of Devotion* (New York: Harper & Brothers, 1941).

James Nayler, *Love to the Lost. 1656. A collection of sundry books, epistles and papers.* (London: J. Sowle, 1715).

Isaac Penington, *Knowing the Mystery of Life Within: Selected Writings of Isaac Penington in Their Historical and Theological Context* (London: Quaker Books, 2005).

William Penn, *Twenty-First Century Penn: Writings on Faith and Practice of the People Called Quakers*, ed. Paul Buckley (Richmond, IN: Earlham School of Religion, 2003).

Hannah Whitall Smith, *The Christian's Secret of a Happy Life* (Chicago: The Christian Witness Company, 1885).

John Woolman, *Journal and Major Essays of John Woolman*, ed. Phillips P. Moulton (Richmond, IN: Friends United Press, 1989).

HISTORY AND BIOGRAPHY

Jervis Anderson, *Bayard Rustin: The Troubles I've Seen: A Biography* (New York: HarperCollins, 1997).

Margaret Hope Bacon, *Valiant Friend: The Life of Lucretia Mott* (New York: Walker and Co., 1980).

Hugh Barbour, *The Quakers in Puritan England* (New Haven, CT: Yale University Press, 1964).

Cherice Bock, "Oregon Yearly Meeting and the Peace Testimony, Part I: Navigating Evangelicalism and Quakerism, 1938–1954." *Quaker Religious Thought* 133 (Sept. 2019): 22–31.

Peter Brock, *The Quaker Peace Testimony, 1660–1914* (York, UK: Sessions Book Trust, 1990).

Emma Condori Mamami, *Quakers in Bolivia: The Early History of Bolivian Friends* (La Paz, Bolivia: Publicaciones CALA, 2017).

Carol Faulkner, *Lucretia Mott's Heresy: Abolition and Women's Rights* (Philadelphia: University of Pennsylvania Press, 2011).

J. William Frost, "Our Deeds Carry Our Message: The Early History of the American Friends Service Committee," *Quaker History*, 81:1 (1992): 1–41.

Douglas Gwyn, *The Covenant Crucified: Quakers and the Rise of Capitalism* (Wallingford, PA: Pendle Hill Publications, 1995).

Thomas Hamm, *The Transformation of American Quakerism: Orthodox Friends, 1800–1907* (Bloomington, IN: Indiana University Press, 1988).

Nancy A. Hewitt, *Radical Friend: Amy Kirby Post and Her Activist Worlds* (Chapel Hill, NC: University of North Carolina Press, 2018).

Larry Ingle, *First among Friends: George Fox and the Creation of Quakerism* (New York: Oxford University Press, 1994).

Larry Ingle, *Nixon's First Cover-Up: The Religious Life of a Quaker President* (Columbia, MO: University of Missouri Press, 2015).

Larry Ingle, *Quakers in Conflict: The Hicksite Reformation* (Knoxville, TN: University of Tennessee Press, 1986).

Maurice Jackson, *Let This Voice Be Heard: Anthony Benezet, Father of Atlantic Abolitionism* (Philadelphia: University of Pennsylvania Press, 2009).

Rebecca Larson, *Daughters of Light: Quaker Women Preaching and Prophesying in the Colonies and Abroad: 1700–1775* (Chapel Hill, NC: University of North Carolina Press, 1999).

Donna McDonald and Vanessa Julye, *Fit for Freedom, Not for Friendship: Quakers, African Americans, and the Myth of Racial Justice* (Philadelphia: Friends General Conference, 2009).

Clyde Milner, *With Good Intentions: Quaker Work among the Pawnees, Otos, and Omahas in the 1870s* (Lincoln, NE: University of Nebraska Press, 1982).

Rosemary Moore, *The Light in Their Consciences: Early Quakers in Britain, 1646–1666* (University Park, PA: Pennsylvania State University Press, 2000).

Andrew Murphy, *William Penn: A Biography* (New York: Oxford University Press, 2018).

Gary Nash, *Quakers and Politics: Pennsylvania, 1680–1726* (Princeton, NJ: Princeton University Press, 1968).

Gary Nash, *Warner Mifflin, Unflinching Quaker Abolitionist* (Philadelphia: University of Pennsylvania Press, 2017).

Geoffrey Plank, *John Wollman's Path to the Peaceable Kingdom* (Philadelphia: University of Pennsylvania Press, 2012).

James Proud, *William Penn's 'Holy Experiment': Quaker Truth in Pennsylvania, 1682–1781* (San Francisco, CA: Inner Light Books, 2019).

Ane Marie Bak Rasmussen, *A History of the Quaker Movement in Africa* (London: British Academic Press, 1995).

Marcus Rediker, *Benjamin Lay: The Fearless Quaker Dwarf Who Became the First Revolutionary Abolitionist* (Boston: Beacon Press, 2017).

Hans A. Schmidt, *Quakers and Nazis: Inner Light in Outer Darkness* (Columbia, MO: University of Missouri Press, 1997).

Thomas Slaughter, *The Beautiful Mind of John Woolman: Apostle of Abolitionism* (New York: Hill and Wang, 2008).

Jean R. Soderlund, *Quakers and Slavery: A Divided Spirit* (Princeton, NJ: Princeton University Press, 1985).

Nancy J. Thomas, *A Long Walk, A Gradual Ascent: The Story of the Bolivian Friends Church in Its Context of Conflict* (Eugene, OR: Wipf and Stock, 2019).

Frederick Tolles, *Meetinghouse and Counting House: The Quaker Merchants of Colonial Philadelphia, 1680–1763* (Chapel Hill, NC: University of North Carolina Press, 1948).

Christine Trevett, *Women and Quakerism in the Seventeenth Century* (York, UK: Sessions Book Trust, 1991).

James Walvin, *The Quakers: Money and Morals* (London: John Murray, 1997).

Meredith Baldwin Weddle, *Walking in the Way of Peace: Quaker Pacifism in the Seventeenth Century* (New York: Oxford University Press, 2001).

QUAKERISM IN PRACTICE

Margery Post Abbott, *To Be Broken and Tender: A Quaker Theology for Today* (San Francisco, CA: Friends Bulletin Corporation, 2010).

Margery Post Abbott, *Walk Humbly, Serve Boldly: Modern Quakers as Everyday Prophets* (San Francisco, CA: Inner Light Books, 2018).

Margery Post Abbott and Peggy Senger Parsons, *Walk Worthy of Your Calling: Quakers and the Traveling Ministry* (Richmond, IN: Friends United Press, 2004).

Allan W. Austin, *Quaker Brotherhood: International Activism and the American Friends Service Committee, 1917–1950* (Urbana, IL: University of Illinois Press, 2012).

Marian Baker and Priscilla Makhino, *Travelling in Ministry: Let Your Light Shine*, Hill of Vision Pamphlet 5 (Kaimosi, Kenya: Kaimosi Friends Press, 2009).

Being Salt and Light: Friends Living the Kingdom of God in a Broken World, Sixth World Conference of Friends, Kabarak University, Nakuru, Kenya, April 17–25, 2012 (London: Friends World Committee for Consultation, 2013).

Elise Boulding, *One Small Plot of Heaven: Reflections on Famiy Life by a Quaker Sociologist* (Wallingford, PA: Pendle Hill Publications, 1989).

David Bucura, *The Quaker Testimony of Integrity in the African Context* (Kaimosi, Kenya: Kaimosi Friends Press, 2013).

Jane Calvert, "Political Obligation and Civil Dissent." *Quaker Religious Thought* (Nov.2006): 67–78.

Jim Corbett, *Goatwalking* (New York: Penguin, 1991).

Adam Curle, *True Justice: Quaker Peace Makers and Peace Making* (London: Quaker Home Service, 1981).

Ben Pink Dandelion, *Celebrating the Quaker Way* (London: Quaker Books, 2010).

Brian Drayton and William P.Taber, Jr., *A Language for the Inward Landscape: Spiritual Wisdom from the Quaker Movement* (Philadelphia: Tract Association of Friends, 2015).

Lon Fendall, Jan Wood, and Bruce Bishop, *Practicing Discernment Together: Finding God's Way Forward in Decision Making* (Newberg, OR: Barclay Press, 2007).

Gerard Guiton, *What Love Can Do: Following the Way of Peace, Justice and Compassion* (Northcote, Australia: Morning Star Press, 2016).

Allison Hepler, *McCarthyism in the Suburbs: Quakers, Communists and the Children's Librarian* (Lanham, MD: Lexington Books, 2018).

Emma J. Lapsansky, "Past Plainness to Present Simplicity: A Search for Quaker Identity." In Emma J.Lapsansky and Anne A. Verplanck (Eds.), *Quaker Aesthetics: Reflections on a Quaker Ethic in American Design and Consumption* (Philadelphia: University of Pennsylvania Press, 2003).

Patricia Loring, *Listening Spirituality: Corporate Spiritual Practice among Friends* (Washington, DC: Openings Press, 1999).

Patricia Loring, *Listening Spirituality, Personal Practices among Friends* (Washington, DC: Openings Press, 1997).

Judy Lumb, *Ending Cycles of Violence: Kenyan Quaker Peacemaking Response after the 2007 Election* (Washington, DC: Madera Press, 2012).

Oscar Lugusa Malande, "The Concept of Hierarchy and Doing Ministry in the Church: Evaluating the Roles of Leaders and the Use of Authority in Quakerism," *Quaker Religious Thought*, 133 (Sept. 2019): 32–41.

Zablon Isaac Malenge, *Early Christianity Revived in the Perspective of Friends in Kenya: A Study Guide on the Quaker Faith and Practice* (Nairobi: Star Printers, 2012).

Noah Baker Merrill, "On Paying Attention," *Friends Journal*, Nov. 1, 2009: 17–19.

Ron Mock, *Loving without Giving In* (Portland, OR: Cascadia Publishing House, 2004).

Esther Mombo, "Haramisi and Jumaa: The Story of the Women's Meetings in East Africa Yearly Meeting, 1902–1979." *The Woodbrooke Journal*, 5 (Autumn 1999).

Esther Mombo and Cécile Nyiramana, *Mending Broken Hearts, Rebuilding Shattered Lives: Quaker Peacebuiding in East and Central Africa* (London: Quaker Books, 2016).

Quaker Faith and Practice: The Book of Christian Discipline of the Yearly Meeting of the Religious Society of Friends (Quakers) in Britain (London: Britain Yearly Meeting, 1994).

Oliver Kisaka Simiyu, "Integrity." *Quaker Life*, July/August2001: 10–11.

Ron Stansell, *Missions by the Spirit: Learning from Quaker Examples* (Newberg, OR: Barclay Press, 2009).

C.H. Mike Yarrow, *Quaker Experiences in International Conciliation* (New Haven, CT: Tale University Press, 1978).

Jean Zaru, *Occupied with Nonviolence: A Palestinian Woman Speaks* (Minneapolis, MN: Fortress Books, 1992).

WEBSITES

Friends General Conference: https://www.fgcquaker.org/connect/quaker-finder.

Friends World Committee for Consultation, Directory of Friends Around the World Online: www.fwcc.directory

Quakers in Britain: www.quaker.org.uk

Quakers in the World: www.quakersintheworld.org

QuakerSpeak: www.quakerspeak.com

INDEX